시 험 에 강 해 지 는

Academy

Grammar

Mate2

시험에 강해지는
Academy Grammar Mate 2

저 자 토마스 방
발행인 고본화
발 행 반석출판사
2020년 8월 10일 초판 1쇄 인쇄
2020년 8월 15일 초판 1쇄 발행
홈페이지 www.bansok.co.kr
이메일 bansok@bansok.co.kr
블로그 blog.naver.com/bansokbooks

07547 서울시 강서구 양천로 583. B동 1007호
(서울시 강서구 염창동 240-21번지 우림블루나인 비즈니스센터 B동 1007호)
대표전화 02) 2093-3399 **팩 스** 02) 2093-3393
출 판 부 02) 2093-3395 **영업부** 02) 2093-3396
등록번호 제315-2008-000033호

Copyright ⓒ 토마스 방

ISBN 978-89-7172-927-4 (13740)

■ 교재 관련 문의: bansok@bansok.co.kr을 이용해 주시기 바랍니다.
■ 이 책에 게재된 내용의 일부 또는 선제를 부난으로 복세 및 빌쉐하는 깃을 금합니다.
■ 파본 및 잘못된 제품은 구입처에서 교환해 드립니다.

시험에 강해지는

Academy Grammar Mate 2

반석출판사
Bansok

학문의 길은 험난합니다. 영어를 잘 하기 위해서는 모든 학문이 그렇듯이 영어에 흥미와 관심을 얼마나 쏟느냐가 중요합니다. 영어 공부는 초기에 누구나 흥미를 갖고 대하게 됩니다. 하지만 문법이 서서히 등장해서 복잡하게 느껴질 때가 닥치게 되는데, 이 때가 영어를 공부하는 사람들에게는 아주 중요한 시기입니다. 바로 영어에 흥미를 갖느냐 갖지 못하느냐가 결정되기 때문입니다.

본서는 다행스럽게도 이런 어려운 시기를 슬기롭게 넘기며 보다 깊은 영어와 영어 문법의 세계로 항해해 나가려는 독자들을 대상으로 합니다. 따라서 누구나 단어에 대한 부담 없이 공부해 나갈 수 있도록 기초 단어 700여 개로 문장을 구성하였고, 문법 내용은 영어를 공부하기 원하는 이라면 누구나 접해서 익숙해야 할 기본 문법을 모두 다루었습니다. 그리고 본서는 문법 항목이 나올 때마다 PATTERN PRACTICE(문형 연습)를 많이 수록하여 같은 내용의 문법을 여러 번 되풀이함으로써 그 문법의 항목만큼은 완벽하게 터득하도록 편집되었습니다. Exercise(연습문제)도 주로 주관식 문제로 구성하였습니다.

영어 문법을 보다 친근하게 접하기를 원하는 모든 이들에게 『시험에 강해지는 Academy Grammar Mate』 1권과 2권이 영문법 총정리를 할 수 있게 해주는 도우미의 역할을 넉넉히 하리라 믿습니다.

저자 토마스 방

이 책의 특징 및 활용 방법

❶ '문장'에서부터 '문장 전환'에 이르기까지 기본 문법에 해당하는 사항들을 모두 설명해 두었습니다. 문장을 이루는 기본 요소에서부터 문장을 어떻게 바꾸는지에 이르기까지 차근차근 공부해 나가다 보면 어느새 영어 문법을 익숙하게 사용하고 있을 것입니다.

❷ 중요한 개념이나 부가적인 내용들은 TIP에 담았습니다. 문법을 공부하면서 개념이 분명치 않거나 더 궁금했던 사항들은 TIP을 참조하세요.

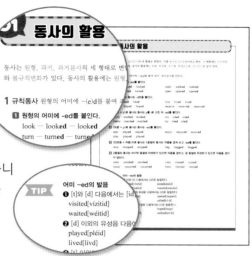

❸ 앞에서 공부한 문법 내용들을 담은 문장들을 Pattern Practice에 따로 모았습니다. 문장들을 읽고 해석해 보면서 공부한 내용들을 상기해 보세요.

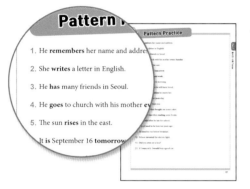

❹ 해석, 영작, 지시대로 바꾸기, 알맞은 말을 써 넣기 등을 통해 공부한 문법 사항을 잘 습득했는지 확인해 보세요. 한 호흡마다 있는 연습문제들로 문법 사항의 습득 여부를 쉽게 확인할 수 있습니다.

❺ 단원에서 학습한 내용을 종합적으로 확인하는 종합문제를 통해서 보다 자유롭게 영어 문법을 사용할 수 있게 됩니다.

목차

머리말 · 4
이 책의 특징 및 활용방법 · 5

Part 1 동사의 시제 Tense
Chapter 01_ 동사의 활용 · 10
Chapter 02_ 동사의 12시제 · 14

Part 2 조동사 Auxiliary Verb
Chapter 01_ 조동사의 종류 · 30
Chapter 02_ 조동사의 특징 · 30
Chapter 03_ 조동사의 용법 · 31

Part 3 부정사 Infinitive
Chapter 01_ 명사적 용법 · 49
Chapter 02_ 형용사적 용법 · 50
Chapter 03_ 부사적 용법 · 51
Chapter 04_ 부정사의 의미상 주어 · 55
Chapter 05_ 원형부정사의 용법 · 56
Chapter 06_ 부정사의 시제 · 59
Chapter 07_ 부정사의 관용적 표현 · 60

Part 4 동명사 Gerund
Chapter 01_ 동명사의 용법 · 69
Chapter 02_ 동명사의 의미상 주어 · 70
Chapter 03_ 동명사의 시제 · 71
Chapter 04_ 동명사와 부정사 · 74
Chapter 05_ 동명사의 관용적 표현 · 75

Part 5 분사 Participle
Chapter 01_ 분사의 용법 · 83
Chapter 02_ 분사구문 · 88
Chapter 03_ 분사구분의 용법 · 89
Chapter 04_ 분사구문의 시제 · 90
Chapter 05_ 주의해야 할 분사구문 · 91

Part 6 태 Voice
Chapter 01_ 수동태의 시제 · 99
Chapter 02_ 문형에 따른 수동태 · 100
Chapter 03_ 문장의 종류에 따른 수동태 · 101
Chapter 04_ 주의해야 할 수동태 · 103

Part 7 가정법 Subjunctive Mood
Chapter 01_ 법의 종류 · 113
Chapter 02_ 가정법의 종류 · 116
Chapter 03_ 주의해야 할 가정법 · 118

Part 8 화법 Narration
Chapter 01_ 수의 일치 · 127
Chapter 02_ 시제의 일치 · 128
Chapter 03_ 화법 · 132

Part 9 접속사 Conjunction
Chapter 01_ 등위접속사 · 145
Chapter 02_ 종속접속사 · 149

Part 10 문장 전환 Transformation of Sentences
Chapter 01_ 문장 전환 · 161

해답 · 193

Part 1

동사의 시제

Tense

동사의 활용

동사는 원형, 과거, 과거분사의 세 형태로 변한다. 이를 동사의 3주요형이라고 한다. 그 변화에는 규칙변화와 불규칙변화가 있다. 동사의 활용에는 원형, 현재형, 과거형, 현재분사형, 과거분사형 등이 있다.

1 규칙동사 원형의 어미에 -(e)d를 붙여 과거, 과거분사를 만든다.

1 원형의 어미에 -ed를 붙인다.

look — look**ed** — look**ed**   walk — walk**ed** — walk**ed**

turn — turn**ed** — turn**ed**   open — open**ed** — open**ed**

2 -e로 끝나는 동사는 -d만을 붙인다.

like — like**d** — like**d**   live — live**d** — live**d**

hope — hope**d** — hope**d**   receive — receive**d** — receive**d**

3 〈자음 + y〉로 끝나는 동사는 y를 i로 고친 뒤 -ed를 붙인다.

study —stud**ied** —stud**ied**   cry —cr**ied** —cr**ied**

marry —marr**ied** —marr**ied**   try —tr**ied** —tr**ied**

4 〈모음 + y〉로 끝나는 동사는 -ed를 붙인다.

stay — stay**ed** — stay**ed**   enjoy — enjoy**ed** — enjoy**ed**

play — play**ed** — play**ed**

5 〈단모음 + 자음〉으로 끝나는 1음절의 동사는 자음을 겹쳐 쓰고 -ed를 붙인다.

stop — stop**ped** — stop**ped**   beg — beg**ged** — beg**ged**

6 2음절의 동사는 마지막 음절에 악센트가 있으면 자음을 겹치고, 앞 음절에 악센트가 있으면 자음을 겹치지 않는다.

omit — omit**ted** — omit**ted**   visit — visit**ed** — visit**ed**

occur — occur**red** — occur**red**   limit — limit**ed** — limit**ed**

어미 -ed의 발음

❶ [t]와 [d] 다음에서는 [id]로 발음한다.

visited[vízitid]   ended[éndid]

waited[wéitid]   mended[méndid]

❷ [d] 이외의 유성음 다음에서는 [d]로 발음한다.

played[pléid]   opened[óupənd]

lived[lívd]   called[kɔ́:ld]

❸ [t] 이외의 무성음 다음에서는 [t]로 발음한다.

looked[lúkt]   hoped[hóupt]

stopped[stápt]   walked[wɔ́:kt]

2 불규칙동사 과거형, 과거분사형이 불규칙하게 변하는 동사로 일상생활에 흔히 쓰이므로 반드시 암기해
야한다.

1 be동사의 변화

am — was — been   is — was — been
are — were — been

2 have동사의 변화

have — had — had   has — had — had

3 조동사의 변화

can — could   will — would
may — might   shall — should

4 일반동사의 변화

① A — A — A형

cut — cut — cut   read — read — read
put — put — put   hurt — hurt — hurt
hit — hit — hit   set — set — set

② A — B — B형

say — said — said   buy — bought — bought
hear — heard — heard   catch — caught — caught
meet — met — met   teach — taught — taught
make — made — made   find — found — found
sell — sold — sold   send — sent — sent
keep — kept — kept   fight — fought — fought
sleep — slept — slept   lead — led — led

③ A — B — C형

do   did — done   drive — drove — driven
eat — ate — eaten   ring — rang — rung
see — saw — seen   speak — spoke — spoken
know — knew — known   wear — wore — worn
take — took — taken   rise — rose — risen
write - wrote — written   tear — tore — torn
begin — began — begun   break — broke — broken
grow — grew — grown   fly — flew — flown

5 혼동하기 쉬운 동사의 변화

lie — lied — lied (거짓말하다)
lie — lay — lain [눕다: 자동사]
lay — laid — laid [눕히다: 타동사]

```
┌ find — found — found (찾아내다)
└ found — founded — founded (설립하다)

┌ become — became — become (~이 되다)
└ welcome — welcomed — welcomed (환영하다)

┌ wind — wound — wound (감다)
└ wound — wounded — wounded (상처 입히다)

┌ hang — hung — hung (걸다)
└ hang — hanged — hanged (교수형에 처하다)
```

3 현재분사 (동명사) 만드는 법 동사의 원형에 -ing를 붙인다.

1 동사의 원형에 -ing를 붙인다.

paly — play**ing**	tell — tel**ling**
read — rea**ding**	study — study**ing**

2 -e로 끝나는 동사는 e를 빼고 -ing를 붙인다.

come — com**ing**	write — writ**ing**
give — giv**ing**	live — liv**ing**

3 -ie로 끝나는 동사는 ie를 y로 고쳐서 -ing를 붙인다.

lie — l**ying**	die — d**ying**

4 〈단모음 + 자음〉으로 끝나는 단음절의 동사는 끝자음을 겹치고 -ing를 붙인다.

run — run**ning**	stop — stop**ping**
cut — cut**ting**	swim — swim**ming**

5 〈단모음 + 자음〉으로 끝나는 2음절의 동사로 마지막 음절에 악센트가 있으면 자음을 겹치고 -ing를 붙인다.

begin — begin**ning**	occur — occur**ring**
cf. visit — visit**ing**	

연습문제

1. 다음 동사의 과거, 과거분사형을 ( ) 안에 써 넣으시오.

(1) play   (   ) (   )

(2) live   (   ) (   )

(3) study   (   ) (   )

(4) stop   (   ) (   )

(5) visit   (   ) (   )

(6) become   (   ) (   )

(7) welcome   (   ) (   )

(8) say   (   ) (   )

(9) write   (   ) (   )

(10) read   (   ) (   )

(11) lie   (   ) (   )

(12) lay   (   ) (   )

(13) find   (   ) (   )

(14) found   (   ) (   )

(15) am   (   ) (   )

(16) are   (   ) (   )

(17) is   (   ) (   )

(18) have   (   ) (   )

(19) has   (   ) (   )

(20) make   (   ) (   )

2. 다음 동사의 현재분사형을 ( ) 안에 써 넣으시오.

(1) play   (   )

(2) study   (   )

(3) come   (   )

(4) lie   (   )

(5) run   (   )

(6) begin   (   )

(7) visit   (   )

(8) write   (   )

(9) swim   (   )

(10) die   (   )

동사의 12시제

1. I write a book. [현재]	나는 책을 쓴다.
2. I wrote a book. [과거]	나는 책을 썼다.
3. I will write a book. [미래]	나는 책을 쓸 것이다.
4. I have written a book. [현재완료]	나는 책을 다 썼다.
5. I had written a book. [과거완료]	나는 책을 다 썼었다.
6. I will have written a book. [미래완료]	나는 책을 다 써놓을 것이다.
7. I am writing a book. [현재진행]	나는 책을 쓰고 있다.
8. I was writing a book. [과거진행]	나는 책을 쓰고 있었다.
9. I will be writing a book. [미래진행]	나는 책을 쓰고 있을 것이다.
10. I have been writing a book. [현재완료진행]	나는 죽 책을 쓰고 있다.
11. I had been writing a book. [과거완료진행]	나는 그때까지 죽 책을 쓰고 있었다.
12. I will have been writing a book. [미래완료진행]	나는 그때까지 죽 책을 쓰고 있을 것이다.

동사의 동작이나 상태의 일어난 때에 따라 여러 가지 형태가 있다. 이를 동사의 시제라고 한다. 동사의 시제에는 12시제가 있으며 그 중에서 현재, 과거, 미래를 기본 시제라고 한다.

1 기본 시제 현재, 과거, 미래를 기본 시제라고 한다.

1 현재 시제 현재의 일만을 표시하는 것은 아니다.

① 현재의 사실, 동작, 상태를 나타낸다.
- She **knows** me very well. [사실]
- She **studies** English very hard. [동작]
- He **is** at home now. [상태]

② 현재의 습관적이고 반복적인 동작을 나타낸다.
- He **goes** to school early every morning.
- I **brush** my teeth before I go to bed.

③ 불변의 진리, 격언 등을 나타낸다.
- The earth **goes** round the sun.
- Failure **is** the mother of success.

④ 미래부사(구)를 동반하여 확실한 미래를 표시할 때 쓰인다. 주로 왕래발착동사 go, come, start, leave, arrive 등이 쓰여 미래 대신 현재형이 쓰인다.
- It **is** Sunday tomorrow.
- My friend **arrives** Seoul next Monday. [확정]
- My friend **will** arrive Seoul soon. [불확정]

⑤ 때나 조건을 나타내는 부사절에서는 미래 대신에 현재형을 쓴다.
- I will leave here when she **arrives** here. [때 부사절]
- If I **meet** her again, I will be happy. [조건 부사절]
    cf. I will tell you **when** he will arrive here. [명사절]
       I will tell you **if** he will arrive here. [명사절]

⑥ 역사적인 현재: 과거의 일을 독자에게 생생하게 묘사하기 위해서 현재형이 쓰인다.
- Caesar **crosses** the Rubicon.

⑦ 현재완료 대용: know, understand, hear, see, write 등의 동사들은 현재 시제로 현재완료의 뜻을 나타내는 일이 있다. 과거에 있었던 일이지만 지금도 유효하다는 것을 나타내기 위한 것이다.

- I **know** him since his childhood. [계속] (어렸을 때부터 그를 알고 있다.)
 = I **have known** him since his childhood.
- Do you **understand** what I said? [결과] (내가 말한 것을 이해하셨습니까?)
 = **Have** you **understood** what I said?

2 **과거 시제** 동사의 과거형을 사용하여 나타낸다.

① 과거의 동작, 상태를 나타낸다.
- I **bought** the book yesterday. [동작]
- My father **was** rich. [상태]

② 과거의 습관적인 동작을 나타낸다.
- She often **came** to see me.
- He **was** usually late for school.
    cf. He **would** often be asleep in class. [과거의 불규칙적 습관]
       He **used to** take a walk every morning. [과거의 규칙적 습관]
       A white house **used to** be near my house. [과거의 연속적 상태]

③ 역사적 사실을 나타낸다.
- Columbus **discovered** America in 1492.
- Admiral Yi Sunsin **invented** the turtle ship and defeated the Japanese.

④ 과거의 경험을 나타낸다. [현재완료의 대용]
- **Did** you **ever** see an elephant?
 = Have you ever seen an elephant?
 ▶▶ 주로 경험부사(ever, never, sometimes, often) 등이 쓰인다.

⑤ 과거완료의 대용: 전후 관계가 명백한 경우에는 과거완료 대신 과거를 쓴다. 주로 after, before, when 등이 온다.
- The train **had started before** we got to the station.
- The train **started before** we got to the station.

⑥ 가정법 과거: 현재 사실의 반대를 뜻한다.

· If I **were** a bird, I **would** fly to you.
  (= As I am not a bird, I can not fly to you.)
· If I **had** much money, I **could** buy a good car.
  (= As I don't have much money, I can not buy a good car.)

3 미래 시제 미래의 일을 나타낸다. 미래 시제에는 단순 미래와 의지 미래가 있다.

① 단순 미래: 말하는 사람의 의지 없이 단순한 미래의 동작이나 상태를 나타내는 말이다. 외적 사정
   이나 자연현상 등에 쓰인다. 미국식 영어에서는 단순 미래에서 인칭에 관계없이 will을
   쓰는 경향이 있다.

	평서문	의문문
1인칭	I shall(will)	Shall I ....?
2인칭	You will	Shall(Will) you ....?
3인칭	He will	Will he ....?

▶▶ 미국식 영어에서는 단순 미래에서 인칭에 관계없이 will을 쓰는 경향이 있다.

· I **shall** be sixteen next year.　　**Shall** I be sixteen next year?
· You **will** succeed if you work.　　**Shall** you leave Seoul next week?
· It **will** rain tomorrow.　　　　　**Will** it rain tomorrow?

② 의지 미래: 말하는 사람의 의지, 결심 등을 나타낸다.

	평서문	의문문
1인칭	I will	Shall I ....?
2인칭	You shall	Will you ....?
3인칭	He shall	Shall he ....?

ⓐ 의지 미래의 평서문: 말하는 사람, 즉 I의 의지를 나타낸다. (~할 작정이다, ~하려고 한다)
  · I **will** read this book by tomorrow.
  · You **shall** go there. (= I **will** let you go there.)
  · He **shall** study hard. (= I **will** let him study hard.)

ⓑ 의지 미래의 의문문: 듣는 사람, 즉 you의 의지를 물을 때 사용한다.
  · **Shall** I open the door? Yes, please.
  · **Will** you open the door? Yes, I will.
  · **Shall** he open the door? Yes, let him open it.

Pattern Practice

1. He **remembers** her name and address.

2. She **writes** a letter in English.

3. He **has** many friends in Seoul.

4. He **goes** to church with his mother **every Sunday**.

5. The sun **rises** in the east.

6. It **is** September 16 **tomorrow**.

7. She **leaves** Seoul **next week**.

8. She **comes** tomorrow morning.

9. I **will** tell you **when** he will leave Seoul.

10. I **will** leave here **when** he meets her.

11. She **wrote** a letter yesterday.

12. He **was** happy that year.

13. My mother often **bought** me some cakes.

14. My father **was** often **reading** some books.

15. He **would** often be late for school.

16. A pool **used to** be here ten years ago.

17. He **used to** run before breakfast.

18. Edison **invented** the electric light.

19. **Did** you **ever** see a lion?

20. If I **were** rich, I **would** buy a good car.

1. 다음 영문을 우리말로 옮기시오.

(1) He knows my name and address. _____

(2) He studies English very hard. _____

(3) She goes to school at six thirty every morning. _____

(4) The sun is larger than the earth. _____

(5) She arrives at home tomorrow. _____

(6) I will go on a picnic if it is fine tomorrow. _____

(7) I will stay here when he leaves here. _____

(8) I don't know if he will leave here. _____

(9) I don't know when he will leave here. _____

(10) She would often sleep in class. _____

(11) He used to take a walk early in the morning. _____

(12) A white house used to be on the hill. _____

(13) Columbus discovered America. _____

(14) He had lunch at twelve. _____

(15) She had many friends in her young days. _____

2. 다음 문장을 영작하시오.

(1) 그는 영어로 편지를 쓴다. _____

(2) 그는 영어로 편지를 쓸 수 있다. _____

(3) 나는 학교에 종종 결석하곤 했다. _____

(4) 오늘은 3월 27일이다. _____

(5) 어머니는 종종 나에게 약간의 사과를 사주곤 하셨다. _____

2 완료 시제 현재완료, 과거완료, 미래완료를 완료 시제라고 한다.

1 현재완료 〈have(has) + 과거분사〉로 나타낸다.

과거의 동작이나 상태를 현재와 관련지어 나타내는 시제로 4가지 용법이 있다.

① 완료: 현재까지의 동작이 막 완료된 것을 나타낸다. | 지금 막 ~하였다

- I have **just** finished the work.
- Have you written a letter **yet**?
- I have **already** written a letter.
- I have not written a letter **yet**.

▶▶ 완료에는 just, already, yet, now 등의 부사가 잘 쓰인다.

② 계속: 현재까지의 동작, 상태의 계속을 나타낸다. | (지금까지) 계속 ~하고 있다

- I have lived in Seoul **for** ten years.
- He has been ill **since** last week.
- **How long** have you been in Seoul?

▶▶ 계속에는 for, since, these days, How long 등의 시간을 나타내는 부사가 잘 쓰인다.

③ 경험: 현재까지의 경험을 나타낸다. | (지금까지) ~한 적이 있다

- Have you **ever** seen a lion?
- I have **never** seen a lion.
- I have **once** seen a lion.
- I have seen a lion **once**.

▶▶ ever는 주로 의문문에, once와 before는 주로 평서문에 쓰인다. once가 문장 끝에 쓰이면 '한 번'의 뜻이 있다. never는 주로 부정문에 쓰인다.

④ 결과: 과거의 동작이 현재에 미친 결과를 나타낸다. | ~해서 (그 결과) ~한 상태이다

- Spring **has come**.
  = Spring came, and it is spring now.

- I **have lost** my watch.
  – I lost my watch, and I don't have it now.

- He **has gone** to America.
  = He went to America, and he is not here now.

주의해야 할 현재완료

❶ have gone to: ~에 가 버렸다, ~에 가 있다 [결과]
  have been to: ~에 가본 적이 있다, ~에 갔다 왔다 [경험, 완료]
  have been in: ~에 있은 일이 있다, ~에 간 일이 있다 [경험]

  · He **has gone to** America. [결과]
  · I **have been to** America. [경험]
  · I **have been to** the station. [완료]
  · I **have been in** America. [경험]
  ▶▶ 1인칭과 2인칭에는 have gone을 쓸 수 없다.
  · I have gone to New York. (×)
  · You have gone to London. (×)
  · She has gone to New York. (○)

❷ 현재완료는 명백히 과거를 나타내는 말(즉 yesterday, ago, last week 등)과 같이 쓸 수 없다. 또 just now, when 등도 쓸 수 없다. 단 just와 now가 따로따로 쓰이면 현재완료에 쓰일 수 있다.

  · I have met her **yesterday**. (×)
  · I met her **yesterday**. (○)

  · My father has come here two weeks **ago**. (×)
  · My father came here two weeks **ago**. (○)

  · **When** have you seen a lion? (×)
  · **When** did you see a lion? (○)

  · She has come back **just now**. (×)
  · She came back **just now**. (○)

  ▶▶ today, this week, lately, just, now, yet, already 등은 현재완료에 쓰인다.
  ▶▶ 현재완료라도 since 다음에서는 과거 부사가 쓰인다.

  · I have known him **last year**. (×)
  · I have known him **since last year**. (○)

❸ 동사가 상태의 계속을 나타낼 때에는 현재완료의 계속적 용법을 쓰고, 동작의 계속을 나타낼 때에는 현재완료진행형을 쓴다.

  · He has been **ill since last week**. [상태의 계속]
  · It has been **raining since last week**. [동작의 계속]

Pattern Practice

1. I **shall** succeed in the future.

2. You **will** get well soon.

3. She **will** be seventeen next year.

4. **Shall** I succeed if I work hard?

5. **Shall** you get well soon?

6. **Will** it rain tomorrow morning?

7. I **will** write the book by next year.

8. You **shall** carry this box.

9. She **shall** teach them English.

10. **Shall** I bring you a cup of coffee?

11. **Will** you bring me a glass of milk?

12. **Shall** he **build** the house?

13. **Have** you **read** the story book yet?

14. He **has already finished** the work.

15. He **has** not **finished** his homework **yet**.

16. **How have** you **been these days**?

17. I **have known** him **for** ten years.

18. She **has been** ill in bed **since** last week.

19. It **has been raining for** two weeks.

20. **How long have** you **been** in New York?

연습문제

1. 다음 영문을 우리말로 옮기시오.

(1) I shall be sixteen next year. _____

(2) You will succeed if you work hard. _____

(3) She will get well soon. _____

(4) I will learn Chinese to know China. _____

(5) You shall carry the bag. _____

(6) He shall buy the car. _____

(7) Will you bring me a glass of water? _____

(8) Shall I give him a cup of coffee? _____

(9) Shall he write a letter right now? _____

(10) Will it rain tomorrow morning? _____

(11) Have you finished the work yet? _____

(12) I have already finished the work. _____

(13) I have not finished the work yet. _____

(14) How long have you been in Seoul? _____

(15) I have lived in Seoul since last year. _____

2. 다음 문장을 영작하시오.

(1) 비가 한 달 동안 계속 오고 있다. _____

(2) 나에게 우유 한 잔 갖다 주겠니? _____

(3) 제가 커피 한 잔 갖다 드릴까요? _____

(4) 당신은 곧 성공할 것이다. _____

(5) 너는 벌써 편지를 다 썼니? _____

2 **과거완료** ⟨had + 과거분사⟩로 나타낸다.

과거의 어느 때를 기준으로 하여 그때까지의 동작과 상태의 완료, 계속, 경험, 결과 등을 나타낸다.

① 완료: 과거 어느 때까지의 동작의 완료 | (그때) 막 ~하였다
   • When I **arrived**, the train **had** already **started**.

② 계속: 과거의 어느 때까지의 동작, 상태의 계속 | 그때까지 계속 ~하고 있었다
   • She **had been waiting** for me two hours when I **came**.
   • He **had lived** in Seoul before he **left** there.

③ 경험: 과거의 어떤 때까지의 얻은 경험 | 그때까지 ~한 적이 있었다
   • I **had seen** a lion before I **visited** the zoo.

④ 결과: 과거의 어떤 때까지의 동작, 상태의 결과 | ~해서 (그 결과 그때) ~한 상태였다
   • He **had lost** the watch when I **met** him.

※ **대과거: 과거의 어느 때 이전에 일어난 동작, 상태를 말한다.**
   He **lost** the watch that I **had bought** him.
   = I **bought** him a watch, and he **lost** it.

3 **미래완료** ⟨will(shall) have + 과거분사⟩로 나타낸다.

미래의 어느 일정의 시간까지 동작의 완료, 계속, 경험, 결과를 나타낸다.

① 완료: 미래 어느 때까지의 동작의 완료
   • I **shall have finished** the work by six o'clock.

② 계속: 미래 어느 때까지의 상태의 계속
   • I **shall have lived** here for ten years by next year.

③ 경험: 미래 어느 때까지 얻을 경험
   • If I go to America again, I **shall have been** there twice.

④ 결과: 미래 어느 때까지의 동작의 결과
   • She **will have gone** to America by this time tomorrow.

3 진행 시제 현재진행형, 과거진행형, 미래진행형, 현재완료진행형, 과거완료진행형, 미래완료진행형 등 6가지가 있다.

1 현재진행형 〈am, are, is〉 + 현재분사〉로 나타낸다. 현재 동작의 진행, 계속을 나타낸다.
· He **is writing** a letter.

2 과거진행형 〈was, were〉 + 현재분사〉로 나타낸다. 과거의 어떤 때에 진행 중인 동작을 나타낸다.
· He **was writing** a letter.

3 미래진행형 〈will(shall) be + 현재분사〉로 나타낸다. 미래의 어떤 때에 진행 중인 동작을 나타낸다.
· He **will be writing** a letter.

주의해야 할 진행형

❶ go, come, start, leave, arrive 등과 같은 왕래발착동사는 진행형이 가까운 미래의 뜻을 나타낸다. 미래 부사가 흔히 쓰인다.

· He **is coming** this evening.
= He will come this evening.

· She **is leaving** Seoul soon.
= She will leave Seoul soon.

❷ 진행형으로 나타낼 수 없는 동사

ⓐ 상태, 계속을 나타내는 동사
be, have, know, like, love, belong, resemble, wear 등
· I **have** a book. (○)
· I **am having** a book. (×)
· She **knows** me well. (○)
· She **is knowing** me well. (×)

ⓑ 지각동사
see, hear, smell, taste 등
· I **see** him at school. (○)
· I **am seeing** him at school. (×)
· He **hears** her sing a song. (○)
· He **is hearing** her sing a song. (×)
▶▶ 예외: listen, watch는 지각동사이지만 진행형이 가능하다.

Pattern Practice

1. **Have** you **ever made** a model airplane?

2. I **have once made** a model airplane.

3. I **have never made** a model airplane.

4. He **has been to** Paris **before**.

5. She **has gone to** London.

6. Winter **has gone**.

7. He **has been to** London.

8. She **has been to** Seoul Station.

9. When she **arrived** at the bus stop, he **had already left**.

10. I **had never seen** a kangaroo **before**.

11. I **have lived** in Seoul **for** ten years since my father died.

12. I **had lost** my car when I **arrived** here.

13. I **shall have read** this book three times by this week.

14. He **is reading** a book.

15. He **was playing** the piano.

16. She **is coming** soon.

17. She **is leaving** Seoul today.

18. He **will be reading** a book.

19. I **read** the book which she **had bought** for me.

20. She **will come** home soon.

연습문제

1. 다음 영문을 우리말로 옮기시오.

   (1) Have you ever been to New York? _____

   (2) I have never been to New York. _____

   (3) I have five times been to New York. _____

   (4) My father has gone to New York. _____

   (5) I have been to the barber's. _____

   (6) She has been ill since last week. _____

   (7) I have lost the car. _____

   (8) I had never seen a lion before. _____

   (9) The train had already started when I arrived at the station. _____

   _____

   (10) He is coming here soon. _____

   (11) She is writing a book now. _____

   (12) He was writing a letter yesterday. _____

   (13) She will be writing a book. _____

   (14) I shall have read the book five times by this week. _____

   _____

   (15) It has been raining for a week. _____

2. 다음 문장을 영작하시오.

   (1) 나는 런던에 가본 적이 있다. _____

   (2) 나는 아버지를 전송하기 위해 서울역에 갔다 왔다. _____

   (3) 그녀는 미국에 가버렸다. _____

   (4) 그는 한 달 동안 앓아 왔다. _____

   (5) 여름은 갔다. _____

종합문제

1. 다음 ( ) 안에서 알맞은 동사형을 고르시오.

(1) I (take, am taking) a walk every day.

(2) I (take, am taking) a walk now.

(3) She usually (goes, went) to school by bus.

(4) She (goes, went) to school two days ago.

(5) They said that the sun (is, was) round.

(6) They said that he (is, was) honest.

(7) I will leave Seoul if he (arrives, will arrive) here.

(8) I will ask her if he (arrives, will arrive) here.

(9) I will leave Seoul when it (is, will be) fine.

(10) I will ask her when he (arrives, will arrive) here.

(11) He (has, is having) lunch now.

(12) He (has, is having) many books in his room.

(13) I think she (studying, is studying) now.

(14) I see her (studying, is studying) now.

(15) The white house (stands, is standing) on the hill.

2. 다음 ( ) 안에 문장의 시제를 써 넣고 우리말로 옮기시오.

(1) She goes to school. ( ) _____

(2) She is going to school. ( ) _____

(3) He has gone to America. ( ) _____

(4) He has been to America. ( ) _____

(5) It has been raining for a long time. ( ) _____

(6) She has lived in Seoul for ten years. ( ) _____

(7) I have been sick since last year. ( ) _____

(8) I lost the watch which my mother had given me. ( ) _____

(9) I shall have finished the work by twelve. ( ) _____

(10) I have never heard such a music. ( ) _____

3. 다음 문장에서 잘못된 곳을 바르게 고치시오.

(1) When have you finished the work?

(2) It shall rain tomorrow.

(3) My mother has arrived here two days ago.

(4) Whom are you loving now?

(5) I have gone to London to meet my father.

(6) She has arrived just now.

(7) I lived here for ten years.

(8) My brother is usually going to school by bus.

(9) He has done the work before I came here.

(10) It rained since last Sunday.

4. 다음 ( ) 안에서 알맞은 말을 고르시오.

(1) It has been raining (since, for) a week.

(2) He has known me (since, for) last year.

(3) I (wrote, have written) a book last year.

(4) I (wrote, have written) a book since last year.

(5) His wife had been killed many years (ago, before).

5. 다음 ( ) 안에 알맞은 말을 써 넣으시오.

(1) Shall I open the window?

　　Yes, ( ).

(2) Will you open the window?

　　Yes, ( ) ( ).

(3) Shall she open the window?

　　Yes, ( ) ( ) ( ) ( ).

(4) Will it rain tomorrow?

　　Yes, ( ) ( ).

(5) Shall I be sixteen next year?

　　Yes, ( ) ( ).

6. 다음 세 문장의 뜻이 같아지도록 ( ) 안에 알맞은 말을 써 넣으시오.

Three years has passed since he died.

---

1. = ( ) ( ) three years since he died.

2. = He died three years ( ).

Part 2

조동사

AUXILIARY VERB

조동사의 종류

1. He **is** reading a book.   그는 책을 읽고 있다.
2. He **has** written a book.   그는 책을 썼다.
3. She **will** come soon.   그녀는 곧 올 것이다.
4. **Does** she write a book?   그녀는 책을 씁니까?
5. He **can** speak Korean.   그는 한국어를 말할 수 있다.
6. You **must** learn English.   너는 영어를 배워야 한다.
7. You **may** go home now.   너는 지금 집에 가도 좋다.
8. You **should** obey the traffic laws.   사람은 교통법규를 준수해야 한다.
9. She **would** listen to music after school.   그녀는 방과 후에 음악을 듣곤 했다.
10. He **used to** go to church every Sunday.   그는 매주 교회에 가곤 했다.
11. You **need** not meet her.   너는 그녀를 만날 필요가 없다.
12. He **dare** not come in.   그는 감히 들어오지 못한다.

조동사에는 3가지 종류가 있다.

1 시제만을 나타내는 조동사 be, have, will, shall

2 부정과 의문을 나타내는 조동사 do, does, did

3 뜻을 가진 조동사 can, must, may, should, would, ought to, used to, need, dare

조동사의 특징

1 조동사 단독으로는 쓰일 수 없으며 본동사를 보조해 주는 구실을 한다.

2 일반동사처럼 3인칭 단수 현재라도 조동사 어미에 −s, −es를 붙이지 않고 본동사는 항상 동사원형을 쓴다. 단, be, have, do동사의 변화는 예외이다.

3 조동사의 부정문과 의문문은 be동사의 부정문과 의문문과 같다. do, does, did를 쓰지 않는다.

조동사의 용법

1 be (am, are, is, was, were)

1 〈be + 과거분사〉 수동태

· The book **was** written by him.

2 〈be + 현재분사〉 진행형

· I **am** reading a book.

2 have (have, has, had)

1 〈have + 과거분사〉 현재완료

· She **has** just written a letter.

2 〈had + 과거분사〉 과거완료

· I **had** never seen her.

3 do (do, does, did)

1 의문문

· **Do** you write a book?

2 부정문

· You **don't** write a book.

3 동사의 강조

· I **do** think that she is honest.

4 대동사

· He studies English harder than I **do**.

· Did you go to school early yesterday?

Yes, I **did**. (= Yes, I went to school early yesterday.)

· She likes music. So **do** I. (= I like music, too.)

5 어순 도치

· Never **did** I see him.

4 can, could

1 능력, 가능 (= be able to + 동사원형) ~할 수 있다

- He **can** play tennis, but she **can't**. [현재]
  He **is able to** play tennis, but she **can't**. [현재]

- He **could** play the violin. [과거]
  He **was able to** play the violin. [과거]

- You will **be able to** speak Korean soon. [미래]
  She has **been able to** finish the work. [현재완료]

  ▶▶ 미래형과 완료형에는 be able to를 써야 한다.

2 허가 ~해도 좋다

- **Can**(**May**) I come in? Yes, you **can**(**may**).
- Yes, you **can**(**may**). [허가]
- No, you **cannot**(**must not**). [금지]

▶▶ cannot은 약한 금지   must not은 강한 금지

3 추측과 의혹 ~일 리가 없다, ~일까

- **Can** it be true? [강한 의혹]
- It **cannot** be true. [부정적 추측]
- It **cannot have been** true. [과거에 대한 부정적 추측]

▶▶ can(능력)의 과거: could   can(추측)의 과거: cannot have + 과거분사

4 의뢰, 부탁 ~해 줄 수 있습니까

- **Can** you open the window?
- **Could** you open the window?

▶▶ Could you ~?는 보다 정중한 뜻을 나타낸다.

5 관용적 표현

① cannot ~ too: 아무리 ~해도 지나치지 않는다.
- You **cannot** be **too** careful to your health.

② cannot but + 동사원형 (= cannot help + 동명사): ~하지 않을 수 없다
- I **cannot but laugh** at his red tie.
- I **cannot help laughing** at his red tie.

Pattern Practice

1. The houses **were** built by them.

2. He **is** writing a book.

3. He **has** been ill since last week.

4. The train **had** already left when he arrived.

5. **Did** you have a good time?

6. I **don't** have a car.

7. I **did** see him at the park yesterday.

8. She played the piano well. So **did** I.

9. She cannot play the violin. Neither **can** I.

10. **Never** did I meet her.

11. She **can** speak Korean.

12. She **could** speak English.

13. She **will be able to** speak Chinese.

14. **Can** I have another egg? Yes, you **can**. / No, you **cannot**.

15. **Can** he be honest?

16. He **cannot be** a doctor.

17. **Can** you bring me a cup of coffee?

18. He **cannot have been** a doctor.

19. You **cannot** be **too** careful in choosing friends.

20. I **cannot but** write her a letter.

1. 다음 영문을 우리말로 옮기시오.

(1) Rome was not built in a day. _____

(2) They were playing tennis in the afternoon. _____

(3) He has been to Seoul Station this morning. _____

(4) He had written an English book. _____

(5) I did meet her at the park yesterday. _____

(6) I got up earlier than he did. _____

(7) I like to listen to music. So does he. _____

(8) Never did I meet her again. _____

(9) She will be able to write a letter in English. _____

(10) Can I use the telephone? No, you can not. _____

(11) Could you bring me some water? _____

(12) He cannot have been a doctor. _____

(13) It cannot be true. _____

(14) You cannot be too careful in driving a car. _____

(15) I could not but laugh at the funny sight. _____

2. 다음 문장을 영작하시오.

(1) 그것이 사실일까? _____

(2) 그것은 사실일 리가 없어. _____

(3) 나에게 당신의 책을 빌려 주실 수 있습니까? _____

(4) 그녀는 피아노를 칠 수 없다. 나도 칠 수 없다. _____

(5) 나는 그의 빨간 타이를 보고 웃지 않을 수 없다. _____

5 may, might

1 허가 ~해도 좋다

· **May** I play tennis?
· Yes, you **may**. [허락]
· No, you **may not**. [약한 금지]
· No, you **must not**. [강한 금지]

▶▶ might를 쓰면 보다 정중함을 나타낸다.

2 추측 ~일지도 모른다

· It **may** rain today.
· It **may not** rain today.
· It **may have been** true.

▶▶ may(허가)의 과거: might
    may(추측)의 과거: 〈may have + 과거분사〉

3 기원 ~하소서!

· **May** you live long!

4 목적 ~하기 위하여 (= **so that** ~ **may** = **in order to**)

· He worked hard **so that** he **might** succeed.
   = He worked hard **in order to** succeed.

5 양보 ~일지라도

· However hard you **may** try, you cannot finish the work.
· Try as you **may**, you never succeed.

6 관용적 용법

① may well(= have reason to): ~하는 것은 당연하다
   · She **may well** be proud of her son.

② may as well(= had better): ~하는 편이 좋다
   · You **may as well** go home now.

6 must

1 필요, 의무 ～해야만 한다

- **Must** I go home?
- Yes, you **must**(= **have to**). [필요]
- No, you **need not**(= **don't have to**). [불필요]

▶▶ must의 과거: had to
　must의 미래: will have to
　must의 반대: need not = don't have to

2 강한 추측 ～임에 틀림없다

- He **must be** a great man. [강한 추측]
- He **cannot be** a great man. [부정적 추측]
- He **must have been** a great man. [must be의 과거]
- He **cannot have been** a great man. [cannot be의 과거]

▶▶ 추측에는 have to를 쓸 수 없다. must be는 과거 시제에도 사용할 수 있다.

- She must be a kind person. (○)
- She has to be a kind person. (×)
- They said that she must be kind. (○)

TIP **조동사의 주의할 점**

may (허가)	(반대)	may not (약한 금지)
may (허가)	(반대)	must not (강한 금지)
may (추측)	(반대)	may not (추측의 금지)
must (필요)	(반대)	need not = don't have to (불필요)
must (추측)	(반대)	cannot be (부정적 추측)
can (가능) (과거)	could	
can (가능) (미래)	will be able to	
must (필요)	(과거)	had to
must (필요)	(미래)	will have to
must (추측)	(과거)	must have + 과거분사 (must be)

Pattern Practice

1. **May** I play baseball here? Yes, you **may**. / No, you **may not**. (**must not**.)

2. She **may be** unhappy.

3. She **may not be** happy.

4. She **may have been** happy.

5. He studied hard **so that** he **might** pass the examination.

6. **However** hard you **may** try, you cannot climb the mountain.

7. You **may well** study English hard.

8. You **may as well** leave here right now.

9. **Must** I go to school now? Yes, you **must**. / No, you **need not**.

10. **Do I have to** go now? Yes, you **have to**. / No, you **don't have to**.

11. You **must** send her some flowers.

12. You **had to** send her some flowers.

13. You **will have to** send her some flowers.

14. My mother **must be** happy now.

15. The late President Lincoln **must have been** a great man in American history.

16. He **cannot be** a doctor.

17. He **cannot have been** a doctor.

18. I **have to** go right now.

19. **Must** I study English? Ycs, you **have to**. / No, you **don't have to**.

20. I get up early **in order to** catch the first train.

1. 다음 영문을 우리말로 옮기시오.

   (1) May I smoke here? No, you must not. _____

   (2) May it rain tomorrow? No, it may not. _____

   (3) We may have much snow this winter. _____

   (4) She may have been dishonest. _____

   (5) I worked very hard so that I might support my family. _____

   (6) However hard you may try, you cannot solve the problem. _____

   (7) You may well succeed in your business. _____

   (8) You may as well go to bed early tonight. _____

   (9) Must I read this book? Yes, you must read this book. _____

   (10) Must she be tired today? Yes, she must be tired today. _____

   (11) It may not rain today. _____

   (12) He may not have been a doctor. _____

   (13) He must be a poet and teacher. _____

   (14) She may have been a poet and scientist. _____

   (15) The late President Lincoln must have worked for people. _____

2. 다음 문장을 영작하시오.

   (1) 너는 여기서 책을 읽어도 좋다. _____

   (2) 내일은 눈이 올지도 모른다. _____

   (3) 그것이 사실임에 틀림없습니까? 예, 그것은 사실임에 틀림없습니다. _____

   (4) 그녀는 성공하기 위해서 열심히 일한다. _____

   (5) 그는 의사였음에 틀림없다. _____

7 would

1 will의 과거 시제
  - He said that she **would** be very happy.

2 과거의 불규칙적인 습관 ~하곤 하였다
  - She **would** often take a walk in the morning.

3 주어의 의지 ~하고자 한다 (= wish to)
  - He who **would** succeed must work hard.

4 정중한 부탁 ~해 주시겠습니까
  - **Would** you give me some water?

5 과거의 강한 거절 아무리 해도 ~ 않았다
  - I gave her some money, but she **would** not take it.

6 간절한 소망 ~하고 싶다
  - I **would like to** go to Seoul.

  ▶▶ would like to는 주로 미국에서 쓰인다. 회화에서는 I'd like to, He'd like to 등이 흔히 쓰인다.

8 should

1 shall의 과거 시제
  - They said that I **should** succeed in the future.

2 의무 ~해야 한다 (= ought to)
  - You **should** respect your neighbors.
  - You **should have respected** your neighbors.
    = I am sorry that you did not respect your neighbors.
  - You **should not have obeyed** him.
    = I am sorry that you obeyed him.

  ▶▶ should have + 과거분사(= ought to have + 과거분사)는 과거의 어떤 일에 대한 유감, 비난 따위를 나타낸다.

3 간절한 희망 (정중한 표현) ~하고 싶다 (= should like to)
  - I **should like to** go home now.

  ▶▶ should like to는 주로 영국에서, would like to는 주로 미국에서 쓰인다.

4 당연, 필요 [이성적 판단] 〈It is + natural + that ~ should〉의 형식
  이성적 판단에 주로 쓰이는 형용사: natural, necessary, important, right, good 등
  이때 should는 해석하지 않는다.
  - It is **natural** that he **should** do such a thing.

5 유감, 놀람 [감정적 판단] 〈It is + strange + that ~ should〉의 형식

감정적 판단에 주로 쓰이는 형용사: strange, surprising, wonderful, curious, regrettable 등 이때 should는 '~하다니'로 해석한다.

· It is **strange** that she **should** say so.

6 주절에 주장, 명령, 기대, 소망, 요구, 제안(insist, order, expect, wish, request, propose)의 동사가 오면 that 이하 명사절에서는 should를 쓴다. 이때 should는 해석하지 않는다. 미국 영어에서는 should를 보통 뺀다.

· He **insists** that she **should** go home quickly. [영국식]
· He **insists** that she go home quickly. [미국식]

9 ought to(= should) 의무, 당연을 나타내며 must보다 뜻이 약하다.

ought to는 두 단어가 조동사 역할을 한다.

· We **ought to** protect nature.
· We **ought not to** go out late at night.
· We **ought to have bought** the house.

▶▶ ought to의 부정: ought not to   ought to의 과거: ought to have + 과거분사

10 used to

1 과거의 규칙적인 습관   ~하곤 하였다

· She **used to** take a walk every morning.

2 과거의 상태 전에는   ~였다

· The pool **used to** be near my house.

3 be used to + 명사(동명사)   ~에 익숙하다

· She **is used to getting** up early in the morning.

11 need, dare 의문문, 부정문에서 조동사로, 긍정문에서 본동사로 쓰인다.

· **Need** he read the book? = Does he **need** to read the book?
  Yes, he **must**. / No, he **need not**.
· He **need not** read the book.
· He **needs** to read the book.

Pattern Practice

1. He **expected** that she **would** succeed.

2. He **would** go fishing on Sunday.

3. Those who **would** succeed must work hard.

4. **Would** you open the window?

5. I gave her a chair, but she **would not** sit on it.

6. I **would like to** listen to pop song.

7. She **expected** that I **should** succeed.

8. We **should** love our country.

9. You **should** finish the work.

10. You **should have finished** the work.

11. I **should like to** go shopping now.

12. It is **necessary** that we **should** love our country.

13. It is **regrettable** that he **should** do such a thing.

14. He **proposed** that she **should** arrive there at six.

15. You **ought to** leave here right now.

16. He **used to** get up at six every morning.

17. The white house **used to be** on the hill.

18. She **is used to** eating Korean food.

19. She **need** not write a letter.

20. He **dares** to see the sight.

1. 다음 영문을 우리말로 옮기시오.

(1) They said that she would be a great scientist. _____

(2) My father would often read a newspaper in the morning. _____

(3) Those who would succeed should work hard. _____

(4) Would you bring me a cup of coffee? _____

(5) I cooked lunch for him, but he would not have it. _____

(6) I would like to listen to music when I am free. _____

(7) They said that I should get well soon. _____

(8) You should have bought a car that year. _____

(9) It is important that we should be careful about our health. _____

(10) He ordered that I should study English. _____

(11) You ought to protect nature. _____

(12) You ought not to have sold the house last year. _____

(13) He used to go to school by bus. _____

(14) A lake used to be here. _____

(15) Mr. Brown is used to eating Korean food. _____

2. 다음 문장을 영작하시오.

(1) 그는 종종 수업 중에 졸곤 하였다. _____

(2) 나는 점심 식사 후에 커피를 마시고 싶다. _____

(3) 당신은 미국에서 돌아오지 말았어야 했다. _____

(4) 사람은 이웃을 존중해야 한다. _____

(5) 너는 오늘 아침에 일찍 일어날 필요가 없다. _____

연습문제

3. 다음 문장을 ( ) 안의 지시대로 바꾸시오.

(1) He can speak Korean. (미래) _____

(2) You must study hard. (미래) _____

(3) You must work hard. (과거) _____

(4) You should do it. (부정문) _____

(5) You ought to do it. (부정문) _____

4. 다음 ( ) 안에 알맞은 말을 써 넣으시오.

(1) May I go now? Yes, you ( ). / No, you ( ) not.

(2) Must I get up early? Yes, you ( ). / No, you ( ) not.

(3) Can I do it? Yes, you ( ). / No, you ( ) not.

(4) Shall I open it? Yes, ( ). / No, thank ( ).

(5) Will you open it? Yes, I ( ). / No, I ( ).

(6) She may ( ) be proud of her child.

(7) You may ( ) well go home quickly.

(8) Shall he come in? Yes, ( ) him come in.

(9) He who ( ) succeed must work hard.

(10) She studied hard lest she ( ) fail in the examination.

(11) She studied hard so that she ( ) succeed in the examination.

(12) You don't have ( ) go to school.

(13) ( ) it be true? No, it ( ) be true.

(14) What you said may not ( ) true.

(15) Was he able ( ) speak French?

(16) She was so honest that he ( ) not make much money.

(17) I would ( ) to go to the mountain.

(18) I ( ) rather die than live in dishonor.

(19) He dares ( ) love me.

(20) He dare ( ) love me.

(21) I ( ) to get up early every morning.

(22) There ( ) to be a white house on the hill.

(23) He is ( ) to teaching English.

5. 다음 두 문장의 뜻이 같아지도록 ( ) 안에 알맞은 말을 써 넣으시오.

(1) You shall carry this bag.

= I will (   ) you carry this bag.

(2) We should respect our neighbors.

= We ought (   ) respect our neighbors.

(3) You should have bought the car.

= I am sorry that you (   ) buy the car.

(4) You should not have met her.

= I am sorry that you (   ) her.

(5) You could make him happy.

= You (   ) able to make him happy.

(6) She need not have hurried.

= She (   ) need to hurry, but she hurried.

(7) She got up early lest she should miss the train.

= She got up early so that she (   ) not miss the train.

(8) He shall carry the bag.

= I will (   ) him carry the bag.

6. 다음 영문을 우리말로 옮기시오.

(1) She would take a walk in the morning. _____

(2) She should have done her homework. _____

(3) There used to be a small house on the hill. _____

(4) It is natural that he should do his homework for himself. _____

(5) I am used to playing tennis. _____

(6) My friend must be very happy. _____

(7) He who would succeed must work hard. _____

(8) You ought not to play the piano at night. _____

(9) I got up early so that I might not miss the first train. _____

(10) Shall I open the window? _____

종합문제

1. 다음 ( ) 안에서 알맞은 말을 고르시오.

(1) You (would, should) get up early this morning.

(2) (Would, Should) you like to have a cup of coffee?

(3) Those who (would, should) succeed must work hard.

(4) It is natural that she (would, should) do such a thing.

(5) He (would, should) often go fishing on Sunday.

(6) He (will, shall) succeed soon.

(7) I (will, shall) succeed soon.

(8) (Will, Shall) you open the window?

(9) (Will, Shall) I open the window?

(10) (Will, Shall) she go to the market? Yes, let her go there.

2. 다음 문장에서 잘못된 곳을 바르게 고치시오.

(1) You ought to not play baseball on the street. _____

(2) Where did he went yesterday? _____

(3) She will can play tennis after school. _____

(4) She was used to eat Korean food. _____

(5) He worked hard lest he should not fail in the business. _____

(6) You were so old that you should not climb the mountain. _____

(7) I would like to seeing her again. _____

(8) Must I read this book? No, you must not. _____

(9) Must it be true? No, it must not be true. _____

(10) He worked hard so that he may succeed. _____

Part 3

부정사

INFINITIVE

1. I like **to read** a book. [명사적 용법]　　　　　　나는 책 읽기를 좋아한다.
2. I have a book **to read**. [형용사적 용법]　　　　　나는 읽을 책을 가지고 있다.
3. I came here **to read a book**. [부사적 용법]　　　나는 책을 읽기 위해 여기에 왔다.

부정사는 문장 속의 역할에 따라 명사적 용법, 형용사적 용법, 부사적 용법 3가지가 있다. 부정사는 본래 동사의 성질을 가지고 있으므로 그 자체의 목적어, 보어, 수식어 등을 취할 수 있다.

□ 부정사의 형태
〈to + 동사원형〉: to부정사(to 있는 부정사)
〈×동사원형〉: 원형부정사(to 없는 부정사)

1 부정사의 용법

1 명사적 용법
① 주어 ② 목적어 ③ 보어

2 형용사적 용법
① 명사 뒤에서 명사를 수식
② 〈be + to부정사〉
　　ⓐ 예정 ⓑ 의무 ⓒ 가능 ⓓ 운명 ⓔ 의도

3 부사적 용법
① 목적 ② 원인 ③ 이유 ④ 결과 ⑤ 조건 ⑥ 형용사 수식 ⑦ 부사 수식 ⑧ 독립부정사

2 부정사 자신이 취하는 어구

1 목적어
· I want to read **many books**. [book은 read의 목적어]

2 목적격보어
· I want to make him **happy**. [happy는 make의 목적격보어]

3 수식어
· I want to get up **early in the morning**. [early in the morning이 get up의 수식어이다.]

명사적 용법

P · r · e · v · i · e · w

1. **To study** English is interesting.
2. I want **to study** English.
3. My hope is **to study** English.

영어를 공부하는 것은 재미있다.
나는 영어 공부하기를 원한다.
나의 희망은 영어를 공부하는 것이다.

명사적 용법은 부정사가 명사처럼 주어, 목적어, 보어로 쓰인다. 해석은 '~하는 것', '~하기'로 한다.

1 주어 ~하는 것은

· **To teach** English is not easy.
  = **It** is not easy **to teach** English.
  cf. **It** is not easy **for him to teach** English.

· **To tell** a lie is wrong.
  = **It** is wrong **to tell** a lie.
  cf. **It** is wrong **of her to tell** a lie.

  ▶▶ to부정사가 주어로 쓰일 때는 보통 'It ~ to부정사'의 구문이 쓰인다.

2 목적어 ~하는 것을

· I want **to teach** English.
· I don't know **what to do** next.
· I think it easy **to study** English.

  ▶▶ 5형식에서 불완전타동사 think, find, believe, make 등은 목적어로 to부정사를 사용할 수 없기 때문에, 목적어 자리에 가목적어 it을 놓고 진목적어 to부정사는 뒤로 돌린다.

3 주격보어, 목적격보어

· To see is **to believe**. [주격보어]
· I want her **to believe** me. [목적격보어]
· I felt her **believe** me. [목적격보어]
· I made her **believe** me. [목적격보어]

Part 3 부정사 Infinitive

형용사적 용법

1. She is not a person **to tell** a lie.	그녀는 거짓말을 할 사람이 아니다.
2. She has a house **to live in**.	그녀는 살 집이 있다.
3. We are **to meet** here at seven.	우리는 7시에 여기서 만날 예정이다.

형용사적 용법은 to부정사가 형용사처럼 명사 뒤에서 수식한다. 이때 부정사는 일반 형용사처럼 명사 앞에서 수식할 수 없다. 또 〈be + to부정사〉의 형태는 예정, 의무, 가능, 운명, 의도의 뜻으로 해석한다.

1 명사 뒤에서 수식 ~할, ~하는

1 주격관계 수식을 받는 명사가 부정사의 의미상 주어가 된다.
- I have a friend **to help** me.
  = I have a friend who will help me.

2 목적관계 수식을 받는 명사가 부정사의 의미상 목적어가 된다.
- I have a book **to read** today.
  = I have a book which I must read today.

3 동격관계 수식을 받는 명사가 부정사와 동격관계가 된다.
- He made a promise **to do** the work.
  = He made a promise that he would do the work.

4 전치사의 목적관계 부정사에 붙는 전치사의 목적어가 된다.
- I have a friend **to play with**.
  = I have a friend whom I play with.

2 be + to부정사

- They **are to meet** here this evening. [예정]
- You **are to obey** the traffic laws. [의무]
- Not a star **is to be** seen. [가능]
- He **was to die** in young. [운명]
- If you **are to have** a good friend, you must be good. [의도]

P · r · e · v · i · e · w

1. I came here **to meet** you.	나는 당신을 만나기 위해 여기에 왔다.
2. I am glad **to meet** you.	나는 당신을 만나서 기쁘다.
3. He must be a fool **to say** so.	그가 그렇게 말하다니 바보임에 틀림없다.
4. He grew up **to be** a scientist.	그는 자라서 과학자가 되었다.
5. I should be happy **to meet** you.	당신을 만날 수 있다면 기쁘겠습니다.
6. This water is good **to drink**.	이 물은 마시기 좋다.
7. She is too old **to work**.	그녀는 너무 나이가 들어서 일할 수 없다.
8. **To tell the truth**, I am not a writer.	사실을 말하면, 나는 작가가 아니다.

부사적 용법은 부사처럼 동사, 형용사, 부사를 수식한다. 다음과 같이 8가지 용법이 있다.

1 목적   ~하기 위하여, ~하려고

· We eat **to live**. (= We eat **in order to live**.)
   = We eat **so that** we **may** live.

2 원인   ~해서, ~하니

· I am happy **to see** you.

  ▶▶ 감정을 나타내는 형용사(glad, happy, sorry, surprised 등)나 동사(smile, weep, rejoice 등) 뒤에 오면 원인을 나타낸다.

3 이유   ~라니, ~하다니

· He must be rich **to buy** such a nice house.
· He cannot be a fool **to say** so.

  ▶▶ 추측을 나타내는 조동사(must be, cannot be) 뒤에 오는 부정사는 이유를 나타낸다.

4 결과   ~해서 ~하다

· One morning she awoke **to find** herself famous.
· She lived **to be** eighty.
· He worked hard only **to fail**.
   = He worked hard. but he failed.

▶▶ grow up, live, awake 등의 무의지 동사 뒤에 오거나 only, never 등을 수반할 경우 부정사는 결과를 나타낸다.

5 조건 ~한다면

· I should be happy **to go** with you.
   = If I go with you, I should be happy.

· You will be punished **to make** a mistake again.
   = If you make a mistake again, you will be punished.

6 형용사 수식 ~할, ~하기에

· This book is easy **to read**.
· The milk is good **to drink**.

7 부사 수식 부정사 앞의 부사를 수식한다.

· She is **too** young **to go** to school.
   = She is **so** young **that** she **cannot** go to school.

· She is rich **enough to** buy a car.
   = She is **so** rich **that** she **can** buy a car.

8 독립부정사 문두 또는 문중에서 문장 전체를 수식하며, 대부분 관용적으로 쓰인다.

· **To be frank with you**, I have nothing.
· **To tell the truth**, he is a writer.
· **Strange to say**, he is not honest.
· **To make matters worse**, her mother died.

1. **To study** hard is important.

2. It is important **to study** hard.

3. It is important **for him to study** hard.

4. **To learn** English is not easy.

5. It is not easy **to learn** English.

6. It is not easy **for her to learn** English.

7. She likes **to listen** to music.

8. I don't know **where to go**.

9. I believe it difficult **to study** English.

10. My hobby is **to skate** in winter.

11. **To see** is **to believe**.

12. I want him **to go** to church.

13. I have many friends **to play with**.

14. I have nothing **to give** you.

15. I have something **to tell** you.

16. I have no house **to live in**.

17. He gets up early **to go** to school.

18. He gets up early **not to be** late for school.

19. He worked hard **not to fail** in life.

20. She was very glad **to see** an old friend of hers.

21. She was very happy **to meet** her husband again.

22. He must be wise **to understand** the matter.

23. She cannot be foolish **to say** such a thing.

24. She lived **to see** her grandchildren.

25. He left his home, never **to return**.

26. He is **too** young **to go** to school.

27. He is **too** weak **to climb** the mountain.

28. This book is **too** difficult **for him to read**.

29. This stone is **too** heavy **for him to lift**.

30. He is strong **enough to** climb the mountain.

연습문제

1. 다음 문장에 쓰인 부정사의 용법을 ( ) 안에 써 넣고 우리말로 옮기시오.

(1) To learn English is interesting. ( ) _____

(2) I want to go to London. ( ) _____

(3) My hope is to swim in summer. ( ) _____

(4) Mom, please give me something to eat. ( ) _____

(5) He went to school to study. ( ) _____

(6) I was surprised to hear the news. ( ) _____

(7) She must be clever to answer such a question. ( ) _____

(8) He grew up to be a great poet. ( ) _____

(9) I should be happy to go on a picnic. ( ) _____

(10) This book is difficult to read. ( ) _____

(11) This book is too difficult for him to read. ( ) _____

(12) This book is easy enough for him to read. ( ) _____

(13) To tell the truth, he is not honest. ( ) _____

(14) It is interesting to learn Chinese. ( ) _____

(15) She is to go home tomorrow. ( ) _____

2. 다음 문장을 영작하시오.
(1) 나는 책 읽기를 원한다. _____

(2) 나는 공부하기 위하여 학교에 간다. _____

(3) 그는 살 집이 없다. _____

(4) 그녀는 친구를 만나서 행복하다. _____

(5) 열심히 공부하는 것은 중요하다. _____

Chapter 04 부정사의 의미상 주어

P·r·e·v·i·e·w

1. I want **to read** this book.	나는 이 책 읽기를 원한다.
2. I want **her to read** this book.	나는 그녀가 이 책 읽기를 원한다.
3. It is difficult **for her to read** this book.	그녀가 이 책을 읽는 것은 어렵다.

부정사는 술어동사가 아니므로 문법상의 주어는 가질 수 없지만 의미상의 주어는 가질 수 있다.

1 문장의 주어와 일치할 경우

· **I** expect **to succeed**.
  = I expect that I shall succeed.
· **He** hopes **to succeed**.
  = He hopes that he will succeed.

2 문장의 목적어와 일치할 경우

· He expects **you to succeed**.
  = He expects that you will succeed.
· He expects **me to succeed**.
  = He expects that I shall succeed.

3 〈for + 목적어 + to부정사〉의 경우

· It is impossible **for her to pass** the examination.
  = It is impossible that she should pass the examination.
  ▶▶ 주로 쓰이는 형용사: impossible, necessary, easy, difficult, natural, worth 등
· There are many books for you to read.
  = There are many books that you should read.
· I stepped aside for her to pass by.
  = I stepped aside so that she could pass by.

4 〈of + 목적어 + to부정사〉의 경우

· It is kind **of you to say** so.
  ▶▶ 사람의 성격을 나타내는 형용사(kind, wise, foolish, clever, bad, good, careful, careless, nice) 등이 오면 for 대신에 of를 쓴다.

원형부정사의 용법

1. I saw her **go** to school.
2. I made her **go** to school.
3. You had better **go** to school.

나는 그녀가 학교에 가는 것을 보았다.
나는 그녀를 학교에 가게 했다.
너는 학교에 가는 것이 좋겠다.

to 없는 부정사를 원형부정사라고 한다.

1 조동사 뒤에 쓰인다.

· She can **speak** English.
· She must **study** English.

2 지각동사의 목적보어로 쓰인다.

· I heard her **sing** a song.
· I felt my house **shake**.

▶▶ 지각동사: see, hear, feel, smell, watch, listen to 등

3 사역동사의 목적보어로 쓰인다.

· I had him **clean** the room.
· Let me **know** your name.

▶▶ 사역동사: make, have, let, bid 등
▶▶ 사역의 뜻은 있지만 목적보어로 to부정사를 쓰는 말: compel, force, allow, get, order, tell 등

· I get him study hard. (×)
· I get him to study hard. (○)

4 관용적 구문에 쓰인다.

· I cannot but **believe** her.
· You had better **go** home now.
· I would rather **die**.
· He may well **be proud of** his child.

5 부정사의 부정 부정사의 바로 앞에 not이나 never를 놓는다.

· I want him **not** to be late.
· You had better **not** go home.

1. **I** want **to swim**.

2. I want **him to swim** in the river.

3. **He** expects **to get up** early in the morning.

4. He expects **me to get up** early in the morning

5. **She** wanted **to go** home soon.

6. She wanted **me to go** home soon.

7. He told **me to read** many books.

8. He asked **me to stay** here.

9. He ordered **me to leave** here.

10. **She** promised me **to study** English.

11. I saw **her swim** in the river.

12. I heard **her sing** a song.

13. I felt **my house shake** last night.

14. I watched **the birds fly off** their home.

15. I made **him get up** early in the morning.

16. I had **the cook cook** curry and rice for lunch.

17. Let **me know** your telephone number.

18. It is important **to study** hard.

19. It is important **for him to study** hard.

20. It is natural **for him to learn** English.

21. It is kind **of him to say** so.

22. It is careless **of her to make** a mistake.

23. He has many apples **for me to eat**.

24. My mother turned off TV **for us to study**.

25. You **had better** not **stay** here.

26. I **cannot but laugh** at him.

27. I thought **it** difficult **to learn** English.

28. I found **it** easy **to read** this book.

29. I make **it** a rule **to get up** early in the morning.

30. I think **it** important **to work** hard.

1. 다음 영문을 우리말로 옮기시오.

   (1) I want to get up early in the morning. _____

   (2) I want him to get up early in the morning. _____

   (3) I want not to be late for school. _____

   (4) He told me to go to bed early. _____

   (5) He asked me to come to the party. _____

   (6) She promised him to write a letter. _____

   (7) I saw her go to church on Sunday. _____

   (8) I saw her going to church on Sunday. _____

   (9) I made her clean the room. _____

   (10) I had him carry the bag. _____

   (11) Let me know your name. _____

   (12) It is difficult to write a letter in English. _____

   (13) It is difficult for him to write a letter in English. _____

   (14) It is kind of you to say so. _____

   (15) I found it difficult to read this book. _____

2. 다음 문장을 영작하시오.

   (1) 나는 영어를 열심히 공부하기를 원한다. _____

   (2) 나는 네가 영어를 열심히 공부하기를 원한다. _____

   (3) 나는 그녀에게 창문을 열라고 말했다. _____

   (4) 나는 그가 편지를 쓰고 있는 것을 보았다. _____

   (5) 그가 영어를 공부하는 것은 쉽지 않다. _____

부정사의 시제

P · r · e · v · i · e · w

1. He seems **to be** rich.   그는 부자인 것 같다.
2. He seems **to have been** rich.   그는 부자였던 것 같다.
3. I expect **to succeed**.   나는 성공하기를 기대한다.
4. I expected **to succeed**.   나는 성공하기를 기대했다.

1 단순부정사   to + 동사원형

1 주문의 시제와 같은 시제 주문의 동사가 seem, appear, prove, be said, be thought, be believed 등이 올 때

- She seems **to be** sick.
  = It seems that she **is** sick.
- She seem**ed to be** sick.
  = It seem**ed** that she **was** sick.
- He **is** said **to be** honest.
  = It **is** said that he **is** honest.
- He **was** said **to be** honest.
  = It **was** said that he **was** honest.

2 주문의 동사보다 미래 시제 주문의 동사가 expect, wish, hope, want, intend, mean 등이 올 때

- I expect **to succeed**.
  = I expect that I **shall succeed**.
- I expect**ed to succeed**.
  = I expect**ed** that I **should succeed**.

  ▶▶ expect(wish, hope 등) + 목적어(to부정사, that 명사절)
       want(like, love 등) + 목적어(to부정사)

- I want to succeed. (○)
- I want that I shall succeed. (×)

- I wish to succeed. (○)
- I wish that I shall succeed. (○)

2 완료부정사   to have + 과거분사 [주문의 동사보다 한 시제 앞선다.]

- She seems **to have been** sick. = It seems that she **was** sick.
- She seem**ed to have been** sick. = It seem**ed** that she **had been** sick.

  ▶▶ 주문의 동사가 seem, appear, prove, be said, be believed, be thought 등이 올 때

Chapter 07

부정사의 관용적 표현

P·r·e·v·i·e·w

1. He is **too** old **to** climb the mountain.
2. He is strong **enough to** climb the mountain.
3. She worked hard **so as to** succeed.
4. She studied **so** hard **as to** succeed.

그는 너무 나이가 많아서 산에 올라갈 수 없다.
그는 산에 올라갈 수 있을 만큼 힘이 세다.
그녀는 성공하기 위해서 열심히 일했다.
그녀는 열심히 공부해서 성공했다.

---

1 too ~ to = so ~ that ~ cannot 너무 ~하므로 ~할 수 없다

· She is **too** young **to** go to school.
  = She is **so** young **that** she **cannot** go to school.
· He is **too** wise **not to** understand it.
  = He is **so** wise **that** he **can** understand it.

2 enough to = so ~ that ~ can ~할 정도로 충분히 ~하다

· He is old **enough to** go to school.
  = He is **so** old **that** he can **go** to school.
· He was strong **enough to** lift it.
  = He was so strong **that** he **could** lift it.

3 so as to = so that ~ may ~하기 위하여 (목적)

· I studied hard **so as to** succeed.
  = I studied hard **so that** I **might** succeed.
· She works hard **in order to** succeed.
  = She works hard **so that** she **may** succeed.

4 so ~ as to = so ~ that ~하게도 ~하다 (결과)

· She studied **so** hard **as to** pass the examination.
  = She studied **so** hard **that** she passed the examination.
· She got up **so** early **as to** catch the first train.
  = She got up **so** early **that** she caught the first train.

5 대 부정사 부정사의 반복을 피하기 위하여 to만 쓰고 나머지를 생략한다.

· You may go home if you want **to**.
· Do you want to go to college? Yes, I want **to**.

Pattern Practice

1. He **seems to be** a writer.

2. He **appears to have been** happy.

3. She **is believed to be** a good teacher.

4. She **was thought to have been** a scientist.

5. I **expect to go** to college.

6. I **expect** her **to go** to college.

7. I **hoped to go** to college.

8. I **hoped to have gone** to college.

9. I **want to go** to America.

10. I **want** him **to go** to America.

11. She is **too** young **to** go out by herself at night.

12. She is rich **enough to** buy a nice car.

13. The book is **too** difficult **for her to** read.

14. The book is easy **enough for her to** read.

15. She is **too** clever not **to** understand the problem.

16. She ran fast **so as to** catch the rabbit.

17. He studied hard **in order to** succeed.

18. He studied hard **not to** fail in the examination.

19. He is **too** weak **to** work.

20. He is strong **enough to** lift it.

21. He stepped aside **for her to pass** by.

22. There are many books **for you to read**.

23. I studied **so** hard **as to** pass the examination.

24. I study hard **so as to** pass the examination.

25. I study hard **so as not to** fail in the examination.

1. 다음 단문을 복문으로 만드시오.

(1) He seems to be poor.

_____

(2) She seemed to be sick.

_____

(3) He seems to have been poor.

_____

(4) She seemed to have been sick.

_____

(5) She is said to be honest.

_____

(6) She is believed to have been a doctor.

_____

(7) I wish to be happy.

_____

(8) I expect to succeed.

_____

(9) I expect him to succeed.

_____

(10) He is too old to go to the mountain by himself.

_____

(11) She is kind enough to tell me the way to the station.

_____

(12) She got up early in order to catch the first train.

_____

(13) He studied English hard so as to pass the examination.

_____

(14) He studied hard so as not to fail in the examination.

_____

(15) I have no friend to play with.

_____

(16) He is the first Korean to fly across the Pacific.

_____

(17) I don't know what to do next.

_____

(18) Do you know where to go?

_____

(19) This book is too difficult for him to read.

_____

(20) It is natural for her to say so.

_____

2. 다음 두 문장의 뜻이 같아지도록 (   ) 안에 알맞은 말을 써 넣으시오.

(1) He knows how to swim.

= He knows how he (   ) swim.

(2) I should be happy if I marry you.

= I should be happy (   ) marry you.

(3) She is too young to go to school.

= She is (   ) young that she (   ) go to school.

(4) He is kind enough to help my mother.

= He is (   ) kind that he (   ) help my mother.

(5) It is time that you went to school.

= It is time (   ) you to go to school.

(6) It is impossible that we should talk with him.

= It is impossible for us (   ) talk with him.

(7) It is difficult that he should study English.

    = It is difficult (   ) (   ) (   ) study English.

(8) It is difficult to meet him.

    = He is difficult (   ) meet.

(9) It is impossible to talk with her.

    = She is impossible (   ) talk with.

(10) He is not a man to tell a lie.

    = He is not a man (   ) tells a lie.

(11) I think her to be honest.

    = I think that (   ) (   ) honest.

(12) I expect him to succeed.

    = I expect that he (   ) succeed.

(13) She seems to be happy.

    = It seems that she (   ) happy.

(14) He seemed to be poor.

    = It seemed that he (   ) poor.

(15) He seems to have been rich.

    = It seems that he (   ) rich.

(16) She seemed to have bought a nice car.

    = It seemed that she (   ) (   ) a nice car.

(17) He is said to be honest.

    = It is said that (   ) (   ) honest.

(18) I expected her to marry me.

    = I expected that she (   ) marry me.

종합문제

1. 다음 ( ) 안에 알맞은 말을 써 넣으시오.

(1) It is not easy (   ) her to teach English.

(2) It is kind (   ) her to say so.

(3) I think (   ) easy to study English.

(4) He has no house (   ) live in.

(5) We are (   ) meet here at seven this evening.

(6) (   ) seems that he is rich.

(7) He is (   ) old to go to the mountain by himself.

(8) She studied hard so (   ) to succeed.

(9) I got up early so that I (   ) not be late for school.

(10) I don't know when (   ) leave here.

2. 다음 ( ) 안에 알맞은 말을 골라 넣으시오.

(1) I want him (   ) science.

    ① to study   ② study

    ③ studying   ④ studied

(2) I saw her (   ) the piano in the room.

    ① to play   ② to be played

    ③ playing   ④ played

(3) I expect that I (   ) succeed.

    ① will   ② shall

    ③ would   ④ should

(4) I was made (   ) the room by him.

    ① to cnter   ② enter

    ③ entering   ④ entered

(5) You had better (   ) home now.

    ① to go   ② not go

    ③ not going   ④ gone

3. 다음 문장에서 잘못된 곳이 있으면 바르게 고치시오.

(1) I heard him to sing a song.

_____

(2) I want him going to school now.

_____

(3) I want that she is going to school.

_____

(4) She is impossible to do the work.

_____

Part 4

동명사

GERUND

1. I enjoy **reading** a book. (동명사 … 명사 역할) 나는 책 읽기를 즐겨한다.
2. I know a boy **reading** a book. (현재분사 … 형용사 역할) 나는 책을 읽고 있는 소년을 안다.
3. I sat by the window, **reading** a book. (분사구문 … 부사 역할) 나는 책을 읽으면서 창가에 앉아 있었다.

동사의 원형에 −ing를 붙이면 명사적 역할을 하는 동명사, 형용사적 역할을 하는 현재분사, 부사적 역할을 하는 분사구문이 된다. 물론 동사의 성질을 가지고 있기 때문에 그 자체의 목적어, 보어, 수식어를 취할 수 있다.

1 형식   동사원형+ing

2 종류

1 **동명사**: 명사 역할
2 **현재분사**: 형용사 역할
3 **분사구문**: 부사 역할

3 동명사의 역할

① 주어   ② 동사의 목적어   ③ 전치사의 목적어
④ 보어   ⑤ 동명사 + 명사   ⑥ 동명사의 관용적 용법

동명사와 현재분사의 구별

❶ 동명사: 주어, 목적어, 보어로 쓰인다.
  현재분사: 형용사로 명사를 수식할 뿐, 명사로 쓰이지 못한다.

❷ 동명사: 전치사의 목적어로 전치사와 함께 쓰인다.
  현재분사: 전치사와는 절대로 함께 쓸 수 없다.

❸ 동명사: 목적 또는 용도를 나타내는 복합 명사이다.
  현재분사: 진행 상태를 나타내고 능동의 뜻을 가지고 있는 형용사 구실을 한다.

동명사	현재분사
a sléeping car =a car for sleeping a wáiting room =a room for waiting *cf.* **명사 + 명사** an English teacher the White House	a sleeping báby =a baby who is sleeping a waiting lády =a lady who is waiting *cf.* **형용사 + 명사** an English téacher a white hóuse

동명사의 용법

P·r·e·v·i·e·w

1. **Writing** a letter in English is not easy.	영어로 편지를 쓰는 것은 쉽지 않다.
2. I finished **writing** a letter in English.	나는 영어로 편지 쓰는 것을 마쳤다.
3. I am fond of **writing** a poem.	나는 시 쓰기를 좋아한다.
4. Seeing is **believing**.	보는 것이 믿는 것이다.
5. I bought a **sleeping** car.	나는 침대차를 샀다.
6. My mother **goes shopping** every evening.	어머니는 매일 저녁 쇼핑을 하러 간다.

동명사는 명사처럼 문장에서 주어, 보어, 목적어로 쓰인다. 또 동사의 역할을 하기 때문에 동명사 자신이 목적어와 수식어를 취할 수 있다.

동명사는 '~하는 것', ' ~하기'로 해석하고, 부정사의 명사적 용법과 같다.

1 주어로 쓰인다.

· **Taking** a walk in the morning is good for the health.

= **To take** a walk in the morning is good for the health.

2 보어로 쓰인다.

· My hope is **speaking** English very well.

= My hope is **to speak** English very well.

3 목적어로 쓰인다.

· It began **raining** in the morning.

= It began **to rain** in the morning.

· She is afraid of **making** mistakes in **speaking** English.

▶▶ 전치사 다음에 동사를 쓰고 싶을 때에는 동명사만을 쓸 수가 있다.

· I am fond of **reading** a book. (○)

· I am fond of **to read** a book. (×)

동명사의 의미상 주어

1. He likes **teaching** English.
2. He likes my **teaching** English.
3. He is fond of her **teaching** English.

그는 영어 가르치기를 좋아한다.
그는 내가 영어 가르치는 것을 좋아한다.
그는 그녀가 영어 가르치는 것을 좋아한다.

1 문장의 주어와 일치할 때

· She is proud of **being** a teacher.
   = She is proud that **she** is a teacher.

· He is sure of **writing** a good book.
   = He is sure that **he** will write a good book.

2 본문의 주어와 동명사의 의미상의 주어가 다를 때

· She is proud of her father's **being** rich.
   = She is proud that **her father** is rich.

· He insisted on my **studying** English hard.
   = He insisted that **I** should study English hard.

동명사의 시제

Chapter 03

P · r · e · v · i · e · w

1. He is ashamed **of being** poor.
2. He is ashamed of **having been** poor.
3. He was ashamed of **being** poor.
4. He was ashamed of **having been** poor.

그는 가난한 것을 부끄럽게 생각하고 있다.
그는 가난하였던 것을 부끄럽게 생각하고 있다.
그는 가난한 것을 부끄럽게 생각하고 있었다.
그는 가난하였던 것을 부끄럽게 생각하고 있었다.

1 단순 동명사 〈동사원형+ing〉 꼴의 동명사이다.

단순 동명사는 술어동사의 시제와 일치한다. 술어 동사의 뜻에 따라 미래의 시제를 나타낼 때도 있다.

· I am proud of **being** a Korean.
  = I am proud that I **am** a Korean.

· I was proud of **being** a Korean.
  = I was proud that I **was** a Korean.

· I am sure of **passing** the examination.
  = I am sure that I **shall** pass the examination.

· I was sure of his **passing** the examination.
  = I was sure that he **would** pass the examination.

2 완료 동명사 〈having+과거분사〉 꼴의 동명사이다.

완료 동명사는 술어동사의 시제보다 하나 앞선 시제를 나타낸다.

· I am proud of **having been** a Korean.
  = I am proud that I **was** a Korean.

· I was proud of **having been** a Korean.
  = I was proud that I **had been** a Korean.

TIP

완료 동명사의 경우 시제의 변화

· is → was(has been)
· was → had been
· has been → had been

· will → would
· shall → should
· can → could

Pattern Practice

1. Would you mind **opening** the window?

2. I know a boy **opening** the window.

3. **Opening** the window, you will be cold.

4. **Studying** English is not easy.

5. He gave up **studying** Chinese.

6. She is afraid of **going** out by herself at night.

7. She is proud of **being** a teacher.

8. She is proud of her mother's **being** a teacher.

9. He is proud of his son's **being** a professor.

10. He is proud of his son's **having been** a professor.

11. He was proud of his son's **being** a professor.

12. He was proud of his son's **having been** a professor.

13. I am sure of **entering** the college.

14. I was sure of **entering** the college.

15. I am sure of his **going** to college.

16. I insisted on her **studying** hard at school.

17. I insisted on his **studying** hard at school.

18. I saw a **sleeping** baby in the room.

19. I bought a **sleeping** car last year.

20. I met a friend in a **waiting** room.

1. 다음 영문을 우리말로 옮기시오.

   (1) Reading many books is good for everyone. _____

   (2) I enjoy reading a lot of books in autumn. _____

   (3) My hobby is reading books. _____

   (4) I am fond of going fishing on Sunday. _____

   (5) I am sure of his passing the examination. _____

   (6) I insisted on your studying very hard. _____

   (7) She is proud of her son's being a scientist. _____

   (8) She was afraid of going out at night. _____

   (9) Seeing is believing. _____

   (10) I want him to pass the examination. _____

   (11) I was sure of his passing the examination. _____

   (12) I am sure of his passing the examination. _____

   (13) I am proud of his having passed the examination. _____

   (14) I was proud of his having passed the examination. _____

   (15) I know a sleeping baby in the sleeping car. _____

2. 다음 문장을 영작하시오.

   (1) 나는 여름에 수영하기를 좋아한다. _____

   (2) 나는 그가 수영하기를 원한다. _____

   (3) 나는 그가 수영을 잘 하리라 확신한다. _____

   (4) 나의 취미는 겨울에 스케이트를 타는 것이다. _____

   (5) 나는 의사였던 것을 자랑스럽게 여긴다. _____

동명사와 부정사

1. I finished **doing** my homework.	나는 숙제하기를 마쳤다.
2. I want **to do** my homework for myself.	나는 혼자의 힘으로 숙제하기를 원한다.
3. I began **learning**(= **to learn**) Korean.	나는 한국어 배우기를 시작했다.

1 동명사만을 목적어로 취하는 동사   주로 동작의 경험이나 결과를 나타낸다.

enjoy, finish, stop, mind, admit, avoid, deny, give up 등

· I enjoy **reading** a book in autumn.
· I stopped **smoking** a month ago.

2 부정사만을 목적어로 취하는 동사   주로 동작의 시작이나 의도를 나타낸다.

want, wish, hope, expect, decide, refuse, agree 등

· I want **to read** a book in fall.
· I expect **to go** to college.

3 동명사와 부정사   둘 다 목적어로 취하는 동사

1 그 의미의 차이가 없는 동사   like, begin, start, love, hate 등

· He likes **reading** a book.
· He likes **to read** a book.

2 그 의미의 차이가 있는 것   remember, forget, try 등

· I remember **seeing** her. [과거의 동작]
   = I remember that I saw her.

· I remember **to see** her. [미래의 동작]
   = I remember that I will see her.

· I tried **making** it. (나는 시험 삼아 그것을 만들어 보았다.)
· I tried **to make** it. (나는 그것을 만들어 보려고 노력했다.)

   cf. I stopped **smoking**. (나는 담배를 끊었다.)
   I stopped **to smoke**. (나는 담배를 피우려고 걸음을 멈추었다.)

Chapter

05 동명사의 관용적 표현

1 go ~ing ~하러 가다

· He **goes shopping** with his wife this evening.

· I want to **go swimming** to the beach in summer.

    ▶▶ go hunting, go hiking, go fishing, go camping 등

2 be busy ~ing ~하느라고 바쁘다

· My mother **is busy cooking** lunch.

3 on ~ing ~하자마자(= as soon as, when)

· **On seeing** me, he ran away.

  = As soon as he saw me, he ran away.

4 cannot help ~ing (= cannot but + V) ~하지 않을 수 없다

· I **cannot help laughing** at his red tie.

  = I cannot but laugh at his red tie.

5 It is no use ~ing (= It is of no use to + V) ~해야 소용없다

· **It is no use talking** to her.

  = It is of no use to talk to her.

6 There is no ~ing (= It is impossible to + V) ~은 불가능하다

· **There is no knowing** what will happen.

  = It is impossible to know what will happen.

  = We cannot know what will happen.

7 be worth ~ing (= be worth while to + V) ~할 가치가 있다

· This book is **worth reading**.

  = This book is worth while to read.

8 be far from ~ing (= never = by no means) 결코 ~아니다

· She **is far from telling** a lie.

  = She never tells a lie.

9 prevent(keep) ~ from ~ing ~에게 ~하지 못하게 하다

· The rain **prevented** me **from going** to the party.

10 Would you mind ~ing ~해 주시겠습니까

· **Would you mind opening** the window?

11 look forward to ~ing ~을 고대하고 있다

· I am **looking forward to seeing** you soon.

Part 4 동명사 Gerund

Pattern Practice

1. I stopped **writing** a letter in English.

2. I stopped **to write** a letter.

3. Would you mind **telling** me the way to the station?

4. I hope **to go** to Mt. Halla this fall.

5. I forgot **sending** a letter to him.

6. I forgot **to send** a letter to him.

7. She began **learning** Korean.

8. She began **to learn** Korean.

9. I want **to go fishing** to the river next Sunday.

10. He **is busy selling** books.

11. **On arriving** here, he went to church.

12. **It goes without saying that** honesty is the mother of success.

13. I **feel like studying** in autumn.

14. My father never comes home **without buying** me ice cream.

15. I **make a point of taking** a walk every morning.

16. I **was on the point of going** out when he arrived.

17. I **never** see you **without thinking** of my mother.

18. **Whenever** I see you, I think of my mother.

19. I **was about to go** out when he arrived at home.

20. **What do you say to going** home?

연습문제

1. 다음 영문을 우리말로 옮기시오.

(1) I want to read a book in autumn. _____

(2) I finished reading a book. _____

(3) I remembered sending her some flowers. _____

(4) I remembered to send her some flowers. _____

(5) I tried learning Chinese. _____

(6) I tried to learn Chinese. _____

(7) I stopped smoking last week. _____

(8) I stopped to smoke. _____

(9) I went fishing to the river last summer. _____

(10) He is busy washing his car. _____

(11) The rain prevented me from going to the party. _____

(12) I cannot help working hard. _____

(13) On seeing me, he ran away. _____

(14) Would you mind opening the door? _____

(15) I never see you without thinking of my brother. _____

2. 다음 문장을 영작하시오.

(1) 나는 어머니와 함께 쇼핑하러 슈퍼마켓에 갔다. _____

(2) 나는 이제 파티에서 친구 만날 것을 잊었다. _____

(3) 나의 어머니는 부엌에서 요리하시느라 바쁘십니다. _____

(4) 그녀는 편지 쓰기를 마쳤다. _____

(5) 그녀는 중국어 배우기를 시작했다. _____

3. 다음 ( ) 안에서 알맞은 말을 고르시오.

(1) I finished (to read, reading) the book.

(2) I want (to read, reading) the book.

(3) I remember (to see, seeing) her last week.

(4) I remember (to see, seeing) her next week.

(5) He likes (to swim, swimming) in the river.

(6) I am fond of (to play, playing) baseball.

(7) I am looking forward to (meet, meeting) him soon.

(8) My hobby is (to collect, collecting) stamps.

(9) I (hope, want) him to go to school.

(10) I (hope, want) he will go to school.

4. 다음 두 문장이 뜻이 같아지도록 ( ) 안에 알맞은 말을 써 넣으시오.

(1) To get up early in the morning is good for the health.

= ( ) up early in the morning is good for the health.

(2) I saw a sleeping baby in the room.

= I saw a baby who ( ) sleeping in the room.

(3) I bought a sleeping car.

= I bought a car ( ) sleeping.

(4) She began to learn English last year.

= She began ( ) English last year.

(5) I am sure of passing the examination.

= I am sure that ( ) ( ) pass the examination.

(6) I was sure of passing the examination.

= I was sure that ( ) ( ) pass the examination.

(7) I am proud of his being a police officer.

= I am proud that ( ) ( ) a police officer.

(8) I am proud of his having been a teacher.

= I am proud that ( ) ( ) a teacher.

(9) I remember seeing her.

= I remember that I ( ) her.

(10) I remember to see her.

= I remember that I ( ) see her.

1. 다음 두 문장의 뜻이 같아지도록 (   ) 안에 알맞은 말을 써 넣으시오.

   (1) On seeing me, he ran away.

     = (   ) (   ) (   ) he saw me, he ran away.

   (2) I could not help laughing him at his red tie.

     = I could not (   ) laugh him at his red tie.

   (3) I never see him without thinking of my son.

     = (   ) I see him, I think of my son.

   (4) It goes without saying that he is honest.

     = It is (   ) to say that he is honest.

   (5) I was on the point of leaving home.

     = I was (   ) to leave home.

   (6) What do you say to taking a walk in the morning?

     = (   ) take a walk in the morning.

   (7) The rain prevented me from going to the party.

     = (   ) of the rain, I could not go to the party.

   (8) She insists on my studying English hard.

     = She insists that (   ) (   ) study English hard.

   (9) There is no knowing what will happen.

     = It is (   ) to know what will happen.

   (10) She is far from telling a lie.

     = She (   ) tells a lie.

2. 다음 문장에서 잘못된 곳이 있으면 바르게 고치시오.

   (1) He wanted going to college. _____

   (2) She started learning English. _____

   (3) I denied to go to the party. _____

   (4) I am afraid of go out at night. _____

   (5) I am sure of reading the book that morning. _____

3. 다음 문장을 밑줄 친 부분에 유의하여 우리말로 옮기시오.

   (1) I tried <u>making</u> it. _____

   (2) I tried <u>to make</u> it. _____

   (3) I stopped <u>smoking</u>. _____

   (4) I stopped <u>to smoke</u>. _____

Part 5

분사
PARTICIPLE

1. I saw a **running** boy.   나는 달리고 있는 소년을 보았다.
2. I found the **broken** window.   나는 부서진 창문을 발견했다.
3. She was **writing** a letter.   그녀는 편지를 쓰고 있었다.
4. He came **running** here.   그는 여기로 뛰어 왔다.
5. She saw me **writing** a letter.   그녀는 내가 편지를 쓰고 있는 것을 보았다.
6. The book was **written** by her.   그 책은 그녀에 의해 쓰여졌다.
7. I have just **written** a book.   나는 책을 막 썼다.
8. **Walking** along the street, I met Mr. Brown.   거리를 걷고 있는 동안, 나는 브라운 씨를 만났다.

1 형식

1 현재분사　〈동사원형+ing〉
2 과거분사　〈동사원형의 과거분사〉

2 종류

1 현재분사　능동의 뜻이 있고 계속의 뜻이 있다.
2 과거분사　수동의 뜻이 있고 상태의 뜻이 있다.
3 분사구문　부사구를 이끄는 구로서 절을 구로 만들 때 분사구문을 사용한다.

3 분사의 용법

현재분사	과거분사
(1) 명사 앞 또는 명사 뒤에서 수식 (2) be + 현재분사 = 진행형 (3) 주격보어와 목적격보어 (4) 분사구문	(1) 명사 앞 또는 명사 뒤에서 수식 (2) be + 과거분사 = 수동태 (3) have + 과거분사 = 완료형 (4) 주격보어와 목적격보어 (5) 분사구문

Chapter 01

분사의 용법

1. I saw a **sleeping** baby.
2. I bought the book **written** in English.
3. He came **crying**.
4. He heard her **crying**.

나는 자고 있는 아기를 보았다.
나는 영어로 쓰인 그 책을 샀다.
그는 울면서 왔다.
그는 그녀가 우는 것을 들었다.

분사는 〈동사 + 형용사〉의 두 가지 성질을 가지고 있어서 형용사 구실과 동사 구실을 한다. 현재분사와 과거분사가 형용사 구실을 할 때에는 한정적 용법과 서술적 용법이 있다.

1 한정적 용법   명사의 앞, 뒤에서 수식하는 용법이다.

1 명사 앞에서 수식   분사가 단독으로 쓰일 경우 명사 앞에서 명사를 수식한다.

· The **sleeping** boy is my brother.
  = The boy who is sleeping is my brother.

· The **broken** cup is expensive.
  = The cup which was broken is expensive.

2 명사 뒤에서 수식   분사가 동사의 성질을 가지고 있으므로 목적어, 보어, 수식어 등을 동반하여 명사 뒤에서 명사를 수식한다.

· I know the boy **playing baseball** on the playground.
  = I know the boy who is playing baseball on the playground.

· I met a girl **reading a book**.
  = I met a girl who was reading a book.

· I like the baby **sleeping in the room**.
  = I like the baby who is sleeping in the room.

· I know a pretty girl **called** Mary.
  = I know a pretty girl who is called Mary.

2 서술적 용법   분사가 주격보어, 목적격보어로 쓰인다.

① 주격보어   불완전자동사의 보어로 쓰인다.
- She **sat reading** a book.
- The soldier **returned wounded** in the battle.

  ▶▶ 분사를 주격보어로 취하는 동사: come, sit, stand, lie, look, seem, return, become, keep 등

② 목적격보어   불완전타동사의 목적격보어로 쓰인다.
- I saw him **reading** a book.
- I heard her **singing** a song.
- I kept her **waiting** so long.
- I found a dog **killed** on the road.
- I cannot make myself **understood** in English.

  ▶▶ 분사를 목적격보어로 취하는 동사: see, hear, feel, watch 등의 지각동사, find, keep, make, have, want 등

주의해야 할 분사의 용법

❶ 지각동사의 목적격보어가 현재분사와 원형부정사일 때 그 뜻의 차이가 있다.
- I saw him **swimming**. [현재분사]: 진행의 뜻을 갖고 있다.
- I saw him **swim**. [원형부정사]: 동작과 사실의 뜻이 있다.

❷ 목적격보어가 과거분사와 to부정사일 때 그 뜻의 차이가 있다.
- I want a book **written** by her. [과거분사]: 수동의 뜻이 있다.
- I want her **to write** a book. [to부정사]: 능동의 뜻이 있다.

❸ 현재분사는 사역동사의 목적격보어로 쓸 수 없다.
- I made her **writing** a book. (×)
- I made her **write** a book. (○)

분사의 특수용법

❶ have + 목적어(사물) + 과거분사
  ⓐ 이익을 볼 때: ~을 시키다
  - I **had my hair cut**.
  = I **got my hair cut**.
  ⓑ 손해를 볼 때: ~을 당하다
  - I **had my purse stolen**.
  = I **got my purse stolen**.

❷ have + 목적어(사람) + 동사원형
- I **had someone cut** my hair. [이익을 볼 때]: ~을 시키다
- I **had someone steal** my purse. [손해를 볼 때]: ~을 당하다

1. I know a **sleeping** baby.

2. I know a boy **playing** baseball.

3. I found the **broken** window.

4. I bought a watch **made** in Korea.

5. He sat **looking** out of the window.

6. He sat **surrounded** by his children.

7. I saw him **reading** a newspaper.

8. I found a man **wounded** by a gang.

9. She was **writing** a book.

10. The house was **built** by them.

11. She has **been** to America.

12. I had my watch **stolen**.

13. I had my watch **mended**.

14. I cannot make myself **understood** in Korean.

15. I heard her **singing** a song.

16. I heard her **sing** a song.

17. The car **made** in Korea is good and cheap.

18. I bought a car **made** in Korea.

19. The man **working** hard will succeed.

20. **Working** hard, he will succeed.

1. 다음 영문을 우리말로 옮기시오.

(1) I met a crying baby. _____

(2) I know a baby crying in the room. _____

(3) I found the broken window. _____

(4) I bought a book written by a poet. _____

(5) I sat reading a newspaper. _____

(6) I sat surrounded by my children. _____

(7) I saw him writing a letter. _____

(8) I saw him write a letter. _____

(9) The building was built by Koreans. _____

(10) She has been to America. _____

(11) She has gone to America. _____

(12) I had my watch stolen. _____

(13) I had my radio mended. _____

(14) I cannot make myself understood in English. _____

(15) I heard her singing a song. _____

2. 다음 문장을 영작하시오.

(1) 방에서 자고 있는 아기는 나의 남동생이다. _____

(2) 나는 자고 있는 아기를 보았다. _____

(3) 그는 울면서 왔다. _____

(4) 나는 그녀가 달리고 있는 것을 보았다. _____

(5) 나는 그녀가 달리는 것을 보았다. _____

3. 다음 ( ) 안에서 알맞은 말을 고르시오.

(1) I saw a (sleeping, slept) baby in the room.

(2) I saw a (killing, killed) dog on the road.

(3) I saw an (exciting, excited) woman in the room.

(4) I saw an (exciting, excited) game in Seoul Stadium.

(5) I saw him (writing, written) a letter.

(6) I saw her (exhausting, exhausted).

(7) I saw the house (building, built) in spring.

(8) I want her (to learn, learned) English.

(9) I want my book (to finish, finished) by him.

(10) He sat (reading, read) a newspaper.

(11) She sat (surrounding, surrounded) by her children.

(12) The man stood (looking, looked) at the map.

(13) The news became widely (knowing, known).

(14) I had the man (make, to make) a speech.

(15) I got the man (make, to make) a speech.

(16) I had my picture (taking, taken).

(17) I had my hair (cutting, cut).

(18) I cannot make myself (understanding, understood) in English.

(19) She kept me (waiting, waited) very long.

(20) The door was kept (closing, closed).

4. 다음 ( ) 안의 동사를 알맞은 꼴로 바꾸시오.

(1) The language (speak) in America is English.　　(　　　　　)

(2) The boy came (run) down the hill.　　(　　　　　)

(3) The (light) Christmas tree is very beautiful.　　(　　　　　)

(4) The (burn) candles on the cake are very beautiful.　　(　　　　　)

(5) This is a very (interest) book.　　(　　　　　)

Chapter 02

분사구문

1. **Walking** along the street, I met her.
2. **Being** ill, he can not go to the party.
3. **Turning** to the right, you will find the building.
4. **Being** poor, he is honest.
5. **Saying** good-bye, she left Seoul.
6. The train leaves Busan at six, **arriving** in Seoul at twelve.

거리를 걷고 있는 동안 나는 그녀를 만났다.
아파서 그는 파티에 갈 수 없다.
오른쪽으로 돌면 너는 그 건물을 발견할 것이다.
가난하지만 그는 정직하다.
안녕이라고 말하면서 그녀는 서울을 떠났다.
그 기차는 6시에 부산을 떠나 12시에 서울에 도착한다.

분사구문은 복문을 단문으로 만들 때 활용하는 구문이다. 즉 부사절을 부사구로 바꾸어 복문을 단문으로 만든다.

1 분사구문 만드는 방법

1 종속절의 주어와 주절의 주어가 같을 때

· As I was tired, I went to bed early.
  ➡ **Being** tired, I went to bed early.

▸▸ 분사구문 만드는 순서
  ① 접속사를 없앤다.
  ② 종속절의 주어를 없앤다.
  ③ 종속절의 동사를 분사(현재분사, 과거분사)로 고친다.

2 종속절의 주어와 주절의 주어가 다를 때

· As it is fine today, I want to go on a picnic.
  ➡ It being fine today, I want to go on a picnic.

▸▸ 분사구문 만드는 방법
  ① 접속사를 없앤다.
  ② 종속절의 주어는 그대로 둔다.
  ③ 종속절의 동사를 분사(현재분사, 과거분사)로 고친다.

Chapter 03

분사구문의 용법

분사구문은 그 뜻의 전후 관계를 보아 때, 원인, 조건, 양보, 계속, 부대상황(동시동작) 등으로 분류된다.

1 때(시간) while, when, after, as 등의 접속사가 주로 쓰인다.
- **Seeing** a police officer, he ran away.
  - ⇒ When he saw a police officer, he ran away.
- **Sleeping** in the bus, I had my purse stolen.
  - ⇒ While I was sleeping in the bus, I had my purse stolen.

2 원인, 이유 as, because 등의 접속사가 주로 쓰인다.
- **Being** busy, I can not go to the meeting.
  - ⇒ As I am busy, I can not go to the meeting.
- **Being** ill, she was absent from school yesterday.
  - ⇒ Because she was ill, she was absent from school yesterday.

3 조건 if의 접속사가 온다.
- **Turning** to the right, you will find the building.
  - ⇒ If you turn to the right, you will find the building.
- **Studying** hard, you will succeed.
  - ⇒ If you study hard, you will succeed.

4 양보 though(although)의 접속사가 온다.
- **Living** in an apartment, I don't know who he is.
  - ⇒ Though I live in an apartment, I don't know who he is.
- **Being** young, she has much experience.
  - ⇒ Although she is young, she has much experience.

5 계속 and의 접속사가 온다.
- The train leaves Seoul at six, **arriving** at Busan at eleven.
  - ⇒ The train leaves Seoul at six, and it arrives at Busan at eleven.
- I watched TV in the evening, **doing** my homework.
  - ⇒ I watched TV in the evening, and I did my homework.

6 부대상황(동시동작) and의 접속사가 주로 온다.
- **Waving** her hands, she left Seoul Station.
  - ⇒ She waved her hands and she left Seoul Station.
- **Smiling** brightly, he shook hands with me.
  - ⇒ He smiled brightly and he shook hands with me.

분사구문의 시제

P·r·e·v·i·e·w

1. **Being** sick, I can not go to the party.	아파서 나는 파티에 갈 수 없다.
2. **Being** sick, I could not go to the party.	아파서 나는 파티에 갈 수 없었다.
3. **Having finished** the work, I have nothing to do.	그 일을 마쳤으므로 나는 할 것이 없다.
4. **Having finished** the work, I had nothing to do.	그 일을 마쳤으므로 나는 할 것이 없었다.

1 단순 분사 〈동사원형+ing〉의 형식

단순 분사는 주절의 시제와 일치한다.

① 주절의 시제가 현재이면 단순 분사의 시제는 현재이다. [분사구문을 부사절로]
② 주절의 시제가 과거이면 단순 분사의 시제는 과거이다. [분사구문을 부사절로]

· Being sick, I can not go to the party.
  ➡ As I am sick, I can not go to the party.

· Being sick, I could not go to the party.
  ➡ As I was sick, I could not go to the party.

2 완료 분사 〈having+과거분사〉의 형식

완료 분사는 주절의 시제보다 하나 앞선다.

① 주절의 시제가 현재이면 완료 분사의 시제는 과거이거나 현재완료이다.
② 주절의 시제가 과거이면 완료 분사의 시제는 과거완료이다.

· **Having finished** the work, I **have** nothing to do.
  ➡ As I **finished** the work, I **have** nothing to do.
  ➡ As I **have finished** the work, I **have** nothing to do.

· **Having finished** the work, I **had** nothing to do.
  ➡ As I **had finished** the work, I **had** nothing to do.

05 주의해야 할 분사구문

1 독립분사구문 주절의 주어와 분사구문의 의미상 주어가 일치하지 않을 때 분사구문의 주어를 생략하지 않고 분사 앞에 둔다. 이를 독립분사구문이라고 한다.

· **It** being fine, **we** went on a picnic.
  ➡ As **it** was fine, **we** went on a picnic.
· **School** being over, **we** played baseball.
  ➡ When **school** was over, **we** played baseball.

2 무인칭독립분사구문 분사구문의 의미상 주어가 일반 사람을 가리킬 때 주절의 주어와 다르더라도 분사구문의 주어를 생략한다. 이를 무인칭독립분사구문이라고 한다.

  ex. we, you, people 등

· **Generally speaking**, Hangeul is the most wonderful letter.
  ➡ If we speak **generally**, Hangeul is the most wonderful letter.

  ▶▶ Strictly speaking (엄격히 말하면)
     Frankly speaking (솔직히 말하면)
     Judging from (~으로 판단한다면)
     Generally speaking (일반적으로 말하면)

3 진행형 분사구문에서 being 생략

· While I was walking along the street, I met her.
  ➡ **Being walking** along the street, I met her. (×)
  ➡ **Walking** along the street, I met her. (○)

4 수동의 분사구문에서 being 생략 [현대 영어에서]

· As the book was written easy, it was sold well.
  ➡ **Being written** easy, the book was sold well. (×)
  ➡ **Written** easy, the book was sold well. (○)

5 분사구문의 부정 분사구문의 앞에 not을 놓는다.

· **Not knowing** where he lives, I can not meet him.
  ➡ As I do not know where he lives, I can not meet him.

6 접속사 + 분사구문 분사구문의 의미를 명확히 하기 위해 접속사를 분사구문 앞에 놓는다.

· **Though living** near her house, I don't know her.
  ➡ Though I live near her house, I don't know her.

Pattern Practice

1. **Meeting** her, I was very happy.

2. **Being** tired, I went to bed early yesterday.

3. **Studying** English hard, you will be an English teacher.

4. **Being** old, he can climb the mountain by himself.

5. **Listening** to music, he made a model airplane.

6. He leaves Busan at seven, **arriving** in Seoul at twelve.

7. **Having breakfasted** as usual, she begins to read the book.

8. **Having finished** the work, she played the violin.

9. **Having stayed** in Seoul for a week, she must start for Busan.

10. **Having stayed** in Seoul for a week, she had to start for Busan.

11. It **being** rainy, we cannot go on a trip.

12. **Frankly speaking**, he is not a lawyer.

13. **Judging from** his accent, he is American.

14. Not **knowing** what to do next, he stayed at home.

15. **Built** on a small hill, the house is beautiful.

16. **Walking** along the street, I met an old friend of mine.

17. **Written** in English, the book is not easy to read.

18. Though **being** young, he has much experience.

19. **Having** met her, I was very happy.

20. **Meeting** her, I am very happy.

1. 다음 영문을 우리말로 옮기시오.

    (1) Reading a newspaper, I was visited by my friend. _____

    (2) Having breakfasted, I went to school by bus. _____

    (3) Being tired, I want to go to bed early tonight. _____

    (4) The train already having left, I could not go to the meeting. _____

    _____

    (5) Getting up early, you can catch the first train. _____

    (6) Living near his house, I don't know him. _____

    (7) I am reading a book, listening to music. _____

    (8) Written easily, the book is read by everyone. _____

    (9) Generally speaking, he is a great man in the world. _____

    (10) It being fine today, I want to go out. _____

    (11) Walking along the street, I met a girl. _____

    (12) Not read, the book was not sold well. _____

    (13) Not writing to her, I was very sorry. _____

    (14) Though living near his house, I don't know him. _____

    (15) The sun having risen, I put out the light. _____

2. 다음 문장을 영작하시오.

    (1) 피곤하므로 나는 오늘은 집에 머물러 있고 싶다. _____

    (2) 오늘은 날씨가 좋으므로 그는 소풍가기를 원한다. _____

    (3) 저녁 식사 후 나는 텔레비전을 보았다. _____

    (4) 그를 보았을 때 그녀는 도망쳤다. _____

    (5) 거리를 걷고 있는 동안 나는 그녀를 만났다. _____

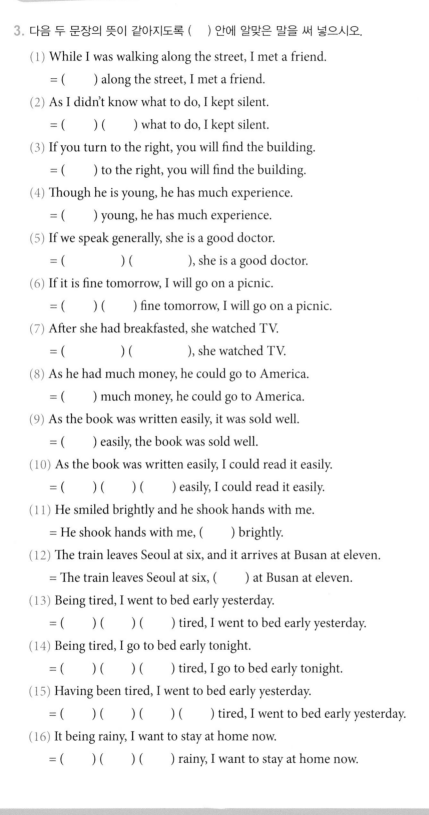

3. 다음 두 문장의 뜻이 같아지도록 (   ) 안에 알맞은 말을 써 넣으시오.

(1) While I was walking along the street, I met a friend.

= (   ) along the street, I met a friend.

(2) As I didn't know what to do, I kept silent.

= (   ) (   ) what to do, I kept silent.

(3) If you turn to the right, you will find the building.

= (   ) to the right, you will find the building.

(4) Though he is young, he has much experience.

= (   ) young, he has much experience.

(5) If we speak generally, she is a good doctor.

= (   ) (   ), she is a good doctor.

(6) If it is fine tomorrow, I will go on a picnic.

= (   ) (   ) fine tomorrow, I will go on a picnic.

(7) After she had breakfasted, she watched TV.

= (   ) (   ), she watched TV.

(8) As he had much money, he could go to America.

= (   ) much money, he could go to America.

(9) As the book was written easily, it was sold well.

= (   ) easily, the book was sold well.

(10) As the book was written easily, I could read it easily.

= (   ) (   ) (   ) easily, I could read it easily.

(11) He smiled brightly and he shook hands with me.

= He shook hands with me, (   ) brightly.

(12) The train leaves Seoul at six, and it arrives at Busan at eleven.

= The train leaves Seoul at six, (   ) at Busan at eleven.

(13) Being tired, I went to bed early yesterday.

= (   ) (   ) (   ) tired, I went to bed early yesterday.

(14) Being tired, I go to bed early tonight.

= (   ) (   ) (   ) tired, I go to bed early tonight.

(15) Having been tired, I went to bed early yesterday.

= (   ) (   ) (   ) (   ) tired, I went to bed early yesterday.

(16) It being rainy, I want to stay at home now.

= (   ) (   ) (   ) rainy, I want to stay at home now.

1. 다음 복문을 단문으로 고치시오.

(1) When he saw a police officer, he ran away.

_____

(2) After he had had dinner, he watched TV and listened to music.

_____

(3) As she is poor, she can not go to college.

_____

(4) As she was poor, she could not go to college.

_____

(5) As it is fine today, I want to go to the mountain.

_____

(6) As he was a doctor, he can solve the problem.

_____

(7) If you turn to the right, you will find the building.

_____

(8) Though he was poor, he was honest.

_____

(9) I arrived in New York at seven, and stayed there for a week.

_____

(10) She shook hands with me and she smiled brightly.

_____

2. 다음 단문을 복문으로 고치시오.

(1) Being busy, I cannot go to your birthday party.

_____

(2) Being busy, I could not go to the meeting.

_____

(3) Having been ill, I can not walk for a long time.

_____

(4) Having no money, he can not buy that car.

_____

(5) It being fine today, I will go out.

_____

(6) Living near his house, I don't know him.

_____

(7) Generally speaking, she is a good doctor.

_____

(8) Turning to the left, you will find the building.

_____

(9) Written in English, the book is difficult to read.

_____

(10) Having been written in English, the book was difficult.

_____

Part 6

태

VOICE

1. I **love** her.　　　　　　　　　　나는 그녀를 사랑한다.
   She **is loved by** me.　　　　　　그녀는 나에게 사랑 받는다.
2. I **made** him a house.　　　　　　나는 그에게 집을 만들어 주었다.
   A house **was made** to him **by** me.　집이 나에 의하여 그에게 만들어졌다.
3. I **made** her a teacher.　　　　　나는 그녀를 선생님으로 만들었다.
   She **was made** a teacher **by** me.　그녀는 나에 의하여 선생님이 되었다.

수동태는 주어가 동작을 받는 형식이고, 능동태는 주어가 동작을 가하는 형식이다.

1 수동태의 형태　〈주격 + be + 과거분사 + by + 목적격〉

2 수동태의 종류

1 형식에 의한 분류

① 3형식 수동태 (3형식 능동태 → 1형식 수동태)
② 4형식 수동태 (4형식 능동태 → 3형식 수동태)
③ 5형식 수동태 (5형식 능동태 → 2형식 수동태)

2 시제에 의한 분류　12시제 중 미래진행 수동태, 현재완료진행 수동태, 과거완료진행 수동태, 미래완료진행 수동태는 쓰이지 않는다.

TIP

능동태를 수동태로 바꾸는 순서

· 능동태 : I love her. (나는 그녀를 사랑한다.)

· 수동태 : She is loved by me. (그녀는 나에게 사랑을 받는다.)

❶ 능동태의 목적어를 수동태의 주어로, 능동태의 주어를 목적격으로 바꾸어 by 뒤에 놓는다.
❷ be동사는 수동태 주어의 인칭과 수에 일치시킨다.
❸ be동사의 시제는 능동태의 동사에 일치시킨다.
❹ 능동태의 동사를 과거분사로 바꾸어 be동사 뒤에 놓는다.

수동태의 시제

P · r · e · v · i · e · w

1. A book **is written by** him. (현재 수동태)
2. A book **was written by** him. (과거 수동태)
3. A book **will be written by** him. (미래 수동태)
4. A book **has been written by** him. (현재완료 수동태)
5. A book **had been written by** him. (과거완료 수동태)
6. A book **will have been written by** him. (미래완료 수동태)
7. A book **is being written by** him. (현재진행 수동태)
8. A book **was being written by** him. (과거진행 수동태)

책이 그에 의하여 쓰여진다.
책이 그에 의하여 쓰여졌다.
책이 그에 의하여 쓰여질 것이다.
책이 그에 의하여 쓰여졌다.
책이 그에 의하여 쓰여졌었다.
책이 그에 의하여 쓰여져 있을 것이다.
책이 그에 의하여 쓰여지고 있다.
책이 그에 의하여 쓰여지고 있었다.

1 현재 수동태 〈주어 + is(am, are) + 과거분사 + by + 목적격〉

· He **writes** a book.
· A book **is written by** him.

2 과거 수동태 〈주어 + was(were) + 과거분사 + by + 목적격〉

· He **wrote** a book.
· A book **was written by** him.

3 미래 수동태 〈주어 + will(shall) + be + 과거분사 + by + 목적격〉

· He **will write** a book.
· A book will **be written by** him.

4 완료 수동태 〈주어 + have(has, had) + been + 과거분사 + by + 목적격〉

· He **has written** a book.
· A book **has been written by** him.

5 진행 수동태 〈주어 + is(am, are, was, were) + being + 과거분사 + by + 목적격〉

· He **is writing** a book.
· A book **is being written by** him.

문형에 따른 수동태

1 3형식(완전타동사)의 수동태 ⟨S + V + O⟩ → ⟨S + V⟩
- A cat **catches** a rat. [능동]
  - ➡ A rat **is caught by** a cat. [수동]
- She **loved** him. [능동]
  - ➡ He **was loved by** her. [수동]

2 4형식(수여동사)의 수동태 ⟨S + V + I.O + D.O⟩ → ⟨S + V + O⟩
4형식의 수동태는 목적어가 두 개 있으므로 수동태도 두 가지 형태가 있다.
- She **gave** me a book. [능동]
  - ➡ I **was given** a book **by** her. [수동]: I.O를 주어로
  - ➡ A book **was given** (to) me **by** her. [수동]: D.O를 주어로
- She **taught** us English. [능동]
  - ➡ We **were taught** English **by** her. [수동]: I.O를 주어로
  - ➡ English **was taught** (to) us **by** her. [수동]: D.O를 주어로

TIP
- He bought me a car.
  - ➡ I was bought a car by him. (×)
  - ➡ A car was bought me by him. (○)
- I wrote him a letter.
  - ➡ He was written a letter by me. (×)
  - ➡ A letter was written him by me. (○)
  - ▶▶ 직접목적어만이 수동태의 주어가 될 수 있는 동사: buy, make, write, send, bring, sell, read, pass 등
- My mother kissed me good night.
  - ➡ Good night was kissed me by my mother. (×)
  - ➡ I was kissed good night by my mother. (○)
  - ▶▶ 간접목적어만이 수동태의 주어가 될 수 있는 동사: save, call, kiss 등

3 5형식(불완전타동사)의 수동태 ⟨S + V + O + C⟩ → ⟨S + V + C⟩
- She **made** me a teacher.
  - ➡ I **was made** a teacher **by** her. (○)
  - ➡ A teacher **was made** me **by** her. (×)
- He **called** me Tom.
  - ➡ I **was called** Tom **by** him. (○)
  - ➡ Tom **was called** me **by** him. (×)
- He **made** me happy. [능동]
  - ➡ I **was made** happy by him. [수동]

문장의 종류에 따른 수동태

1 부정문 〈be + not + 과거분사〉

· She **does not** write a book. [능동]
  ➡ A book **is not written by** her. [수동]
· She **did not** write a book. [능동]
  ➡ A book **was not written by** her. [수동]

2 의문문

1 의문사가 없는 의문문

· **Do** you love me? [능동]
  ➡ **Am** I **loved by** you? [수동]
· **Did** he love her? [능동]
  ➡ **Was** she **loved by** him? [수동]

의문문 수동태를 만드는 방법

❶ 의문문을 평서문으로 바꾼다.
❷ 평서문의 수동태를 만든 후 다시 의문문으로 고친다.
  ex. Did he love her?   ➡ He loved her.
                          ➡ She was loved by him.
                          ➡ Was she loved by him?

2 의문사가 있는 의문문

① 의문사 자신이 주어일 때
  · **Who broke** the window? [능동]
  ➡ **By whom was** the window **broken**? [수동]
  · **Who invented** the radio? [능동]
  ➡ **Whom was** the radio **invented by**? [수동]

의문사 자신이 주어로 쓰일 때 수동태 만드는 방법

❶ 의문문을 평서문의 형태로 바꾼다.
❷ 평서문의 수동태를 만든 후 다시 의문문으로 고친다.
  ex. Who broke the window?   ➡ Who broke the window. [편의상]
                               ➡ The window was broken by whom.
                               ➡ By whom was the window broken?

② 의문사 자신이 목적어일 때

· **What does** she want? [능동]

➡ **What is wanted by** her? [수동]

· **What did** she want? [능동]

➡ **What was wanted by** her? [수동]

의문사 자신이 목적어로 쓰일 때 수동태 만드는 방법

❶ 의문문을 평서문의 형태로 바꾼다.

❷ 평서문의 수동태로 만들고 '?'를 붙이면 된다.

ex. What did he want? ➡ He wanted what. [편의상]

➡ What was wanted by him?

③ 의문사가 의문부사, 즉 의문사 자신이 주어도 목적어도 아닐 때

· **Where does** he buy a car? [능동]

➡ **Where is** a car **bought by** him? [수동]

· **When did** he buy a car? [능동]

➡ **When was** a car **bought by** him? [수동]

의문사가 의문부사일 때 수동태 만드는 방법

❶ 의문사가 없는 수동태를 만드는 방법과 같다.

❷ 의문사를 문두에 놓기만 하면 된다.

ex. When/did he buy a car?   ➡ He bought a car.

➡ A car was bought by him.

➡ Was a car bought by him?

➡ When was a car bought by him?

3 명령문 〈let + 목적어 + be + 과거분사〉

❶ 긍정 명령문의 수동태

· **Finish** the work. [능동]

➡ **Let** the work **be finished**. [수동]

❷ 부정 명령문의 수동태

· **Don't** do it. [능동]

➡ **Don't let** it **be done**. [수동]

➡ **Let** it **not be done**. [수동]

주의해야 할 수동태

1 **5형식에서 목적격보어가 원형부정사인 수동태** 5형식에서 지각동사, 사역동사 다음의 원형부정사는 수동태에서 'to부정사'로 된다.

· I **saw** her **go** out.
  ➡ She was seen **go** out by me. (×)
  ➡ She was seen **to go** out by me. (○)

· She **made** me **go** there.
  ➡ I was made **go** there by her. (×)
  ➡ I was made **to go** there by her. (○)

2 **조동사가 있는 수동태** 〈조동사 + be + 과거분사〉

· I **can** make a model airplane. [능동]
  ➡ A model airplane **can be made by me**. [수동]
  ▶▶ do조동사는 수동태에서 생략된다.

    · I **do** not write a letter. [능동]
      ➡ A letter is not **written by** me. [수동]

3 **〈자동사 + 전치사〉의 수동태** 한 단어처럼 취급한다. 〈자동사 + 전치사 = 타동사〉

· The truck **ran over** a dog. [능동]
  ➡ A dog **was run over by** the truck. [수동]

· He **laughed at** me. [능동]
  ➡ I **was laughed at by** him. [수동]

4 **목적어가 절인 수동태** 두 가지의 수동태가 나올 수 있다.

· They say **that** he is rich. [능동]
  ➡ It **is said that** he is rich. [수동]
  ➡ He **is said** to be rich. [수동]
  ▶▶ say, think, believe 등이 명사절을 목적어로 취할 경우 두 가지 수동태가 나온다.

목적어가 절인 수동태를 만드는 방법

❶ 3형식으로 보고 수동태로 고친다.
❷ by them은 일반 사람을 나타내므로 생략한다.

❸ that이 이끄는 명사절 자리에 It을 놓고 that절은 뒤에 놓는다. (It은 가주어, that절은 진주어)

   ex. <u>They</u> <u>say</u> <u>that he is rich</u>. [3형식: 능동]
       S   V   O

  ➡ That he is rich is said (by them).

  ➡ It is said that he is rich. [복문: 수동]

  ➡ He is said to be rich. [단문: 수동]

5 수동태의 행위자가 일반 사람을 나타낼 때 〈by + 행위자〉를 생략한다   by us, by you, by them, by people 등

- **We** can see stars at night. ➡ Stars can be seen at night (by us).
- **They** speak English in Canada. ➡ English is spoken in Canada (by them).

6 by 이외의 전치사를 사용하는 수동태

- The news surprised me. ➡ I **was surprised at** the news.
- Snow covers the mountain. ➡ The mountain **is covered with** snow.

by 대신에 다른 전치사를 사용하는 수동태

- be surprised at: ~에 놀라다
- be interested in: ~에 흥미를 가지고 있다
- be pleased with: ~에 기뻐하다
- be disappointed at: ~에 실망하다
- be killed with + 도구: ~으로 살해되다
- be known by (판단 기준): ~으로 알 수 있다
- 제품 + be made of + 재료: ~으로 만들어지다 [물리적 변화]
- 제품 + be made from + 원료: ~으로 만들어지다 [화학적 변화]
- 재료(원료) + be made into + 제품: ~을 만든다

- be covered with: ~으로 덮여 있다
- be filled with: ~로 가득 차다
- be satisfied with: ~에 만족하다
- be killed by + 행위자: ~에게 살해되다
- be known to (행위자): ~에게 알려져 있다

7 동작을 분명히 나타내기 위해 be동사 대신 get, become 등이 쓰인다.

- She was tired with the work. (그녀는 그 일로 지쳐 있었다.)
- She got tired with the work. (그녀는 그 일로 지쳤다.)

TIP   **have동사와 사역동사 let은 수동태를 만들 수 없다.**
- I have a book. [능동] → This book is had by me. [수동] (×)
- He let me go. [능동] → I was let to go by him. [수동] (×)

1. Many English books **were written by** him.

2. The tall buildings will **be built** in Seoul.

3. Most children **are loved by** their parents.

4. Many books **are being read by** students.

5. Some flowers **were sent** her **by** me.

6. English **is taught** us **by** Mr. Bang.

7. I **was sent by** God to Korea.

8. She was seen **to play** tennis by me.

9. She was seen **playing** the piano by me.

10. He **was made** happy **by** me.

11. It **is said that** he is a great pianist.

12. English **is spoken** in Canada.

13. A dog **was run over by** a car.

14. The baby **is taken care of by** me.

15. **By whom was** the radio **invented**?

16. **What is made by** her?

17. **Where was** the car **bought by** him?

18. **Was** a model airplane **made by** him?

19. **Let** the door **be closed**.

20. I **am** not **interested in** music.

1. 다음 영문을 우리말로 옮기시오.

(1) She is loved by him. _____

(2) Many plays were written by Shakespeare. _____

(3) A newspaper is being read by my father. _____

(4) She has been made happy by him. _____

(5) It is said that he can speak English well. _____

(6) Mt. Halla is covered with snow. _____

(7) Don't let the work be finished quickly. _____

(8) When was the house sold? _____

(9) By whom was the book written? _____

(10) He is interested in science. _____

(11) The novel is known to everyone. _____

(12) She was seen to go to the mountain. _____

(13) Wine is made from grapes. _____

(14) I am not tired of studying English. _____

(15) I was surprised at the news. _____

2. 다음 문장을 영작하시오.

(1) 쥐가 고양이에게 잡혔다. _____

(2) 나는 나의 선생님에게 사랑을 받는다. _____

(3) 그 책은 그에 의해 쓰여지지 않았다. _____

(4) 영어는 캐나다에서 사용된다. _____

(5) 상자 안에는 많은 사과가 가득 차 있다. _____ _____

3. 다음 ( ) 안에서 알맞은 말을 고르시오.

(1) I was loved by (him, his, he) sister.

(2) The radio was invented by (him, his, he).

(3) She is tired (of, with) walking for a long time.

(4) She is tired (of, with) learning English.

(5) The desk is made (of, from) wood.

(6) Butter is made (of, from) milk.

(7) He is known (to, by) everybody.

(8) A man is known (to, by) friends he gets along with.

(9) He was killed (by, with) a gun.

(10) He was killed (by, with) a robber.

4. 다음 두 문장의 뜻이 같아지도록 ( ) 안에 알맞은 말을 써 넣으시오.

(1) He is building a house.

A house is (   ) built by him.

(2) He has built a house.

A house has (   ) built by him.

(3) He will build a house.

A house will (   ) built by him.

(4) Mr. Bang taught us English.

We (   ) taught English by Mr. Bang.

(5) She wrote him a letter.

A letter (   ) written (to) him by her.

(6) She made me happy.

I was (   ) happy by her.

(7) Who broke the window?

(   ) (   ) was the window broken?

(8) What did he want?

What (   ) (   ) by him?

(9) I made him carry the bag.

He was made (   ) carry the bag by me.

(10) Did he like her?

(   ) she liked by him?

5. 다음 문장을 수동태로 고치시오.

(1) He writes a book. _____

(2) Tom finished the work. _____

(3) He is writing a book. _____

(4) Tom has finished his homework. _____

(5) She gave me a book. _____

(6) I saw him read many books. _____

(7) She made me carry the box. _____

(8) He made me a box. _____

(9) He wrote me a letter. _____

(10) They said that the earth is round. _____

(11) They speak English in Canada. _____

(12) The news surprised me. _____

(13) They laughed at me. _____

(14) She takes care of her baby. _____

(15) Do the work quickly. _____

(16) Did he make a model airplane? _____

(17) Where does she buy a handbag? _____

(18) Who discovered America? _____

(19) What did he want? _____

(20) She never saw a kangaroo. _____

1. 다음 ( ) 안에 알맞은 말을 써 넣으시오.

 (1) She was made happy (　　　) me.

 (2) She was interested (　　　) music.

 (3) He was known (　　　) everybody.

 (4) The mountain is covered (　　　) snow.

 (5) We are pleased (　　　) the result.

2. 다음 문장을 능동태로 고치시오.

 (1) He was loved by her. _____

 (2) Was America discovered by Columbus? _____

 (3) When was a car bought by him? _____

 (4) By whom was the window broken? _____

 (5) He was seen to read a book by me. _____

3. 다음 문장에서 잘못된 곳을 바르게 고치시오.

 (1) I had my radio repair. _____

 (2) I had him repaired my radio. _____

 (3) What did wanted by her? _____

 (4) I am interested with music. _____

 (5) She was seen enter the room. _____

4. 다음 ( ) 안에 알맞은 말을 써 넣으시오.

 (1) They thought that he was a doctor.

   It (　　　) thought that he was a doctor.

   He (　　　) thought to be a doctor.

 (2) They believed that I had been honest.

   It was (　　　　　) that I (　　　) (　　　) honest.

   I was (　　　　　) (　　　) have been honest.

 (3) Don't touch the stove.

   Don't let the stove (　　　) touched.

   Let the stove (　　　) (　　　) touched.

Part 7

가정법

SUBJUNCTIVE MOOD

1. I go to school at seven in the morning. [직설법]
2. Go to school at seven in the morning. [명령법]
3. If you don't go to school at seven, you will be late. [가정법]

나는 아침 7시에 학교에 간다.
아침 7시에 학교에 가라.
만일 네가 7시에 학교에 가지 않으면, 너는 늦을 것이다.

어떤 사실이나 생각 또는 감정을 나타냄에 있어서 사실을 나타내느냐, 명령을 나타내느냐, 가정을 나타내느냐 하는 그 표현 방법을 '법(mood)'이라고 한다. 법에는 직설법, 명령법, 가정법 등 3가지가 있다.

1 직설법   어떤 사실을 사실 그대로 표현하는 문장이다.

1 평서문 ① 긍정문
② 부정문

2 의문문 ① 의문사가 없는 의문문
② 의문사가 있는 의문문
③ 선택의문문
④ 부가의문문
⑤ 간접의문문

3 감탄문 ① How로 시작되는 감탄문
② What으로 시작되는 감탄문

2 명령법   상대방에게 명령, 요구, 금지 등을 나타낸다.

1 직접명령문(2인칭 명령문)
① 긍정명령문
② 부정명령문

2 간접명령문(1, 3인칭 명령문)
① 긍정명령문
② 부정명령문

3 가정법   사실 그대로 말하지 않고 상상, 소원 등을 가정해서 표현하는 문장이다.

1 가정법 현재
2 가정법 미래
3 가정법 과거
4 가정법 과거완료

Chapter 01

법(Mood)의 종류

1 직설법   사실이나 생각 또는 감정을 그대로 표현하는 문장이다.

1 평서문 긍정문과 부정문이 있다.
- She **goes** to school by bus.
- She **doesn't go** to school by bus.

2 의문문 의문사가 없는 의문문, 의문사가 있는 의문문, 선택의문문, 부가의문문, 간접의문문 등 5가지 종류가 있다.
- **Does** she go to school by bus?
- **When does** she go to school by bus?
- **Do** you go to school by bus **or** by car?
- It is fine today, **isn't it**?
- Do you know **where he lives**?

3 감탄문 강한 감정을 나타내는 문장으로 How나 What으로 시작하고 끝에 감탄부호(!)를 붙인다.
- **How** beautiful the lady is!
- **What** a beautiful lady she is!

2 명령법   상대방에게 명령, 요구, 금지 등을 나타내는 문장이다.

1 직접명령문   2인칭 명령문으로 평서문 문장에서 You를 생략한다.
- **Go** home quickly.   **Don't go** home quickly.

2 간접명령문   1, 3인칭 명령문으로 Let으로 시작한다.
- **Let** me know your name.   **Let** me **not** know your name.
- **Let** him go home quickly.   **Don't let** him go home quickly.

3 조건명령문   〈명령문 + and〉: ~해라, 그러면 ~ / 〈명령문 + or〉: ~해라, 그렇지 않으면 ~
- **Study** hard, **and** you will succeed.
  = **If** you study hard, you will succeed.
- **Study** hard, **or** you will fail.
  = **If** you **don't** study hard, you will fail.

3 가정법   사실 그대로 말하지 않고 상상, 소원 등을 가정해서 표현하는 문장이다.

1 가정법 현재   If it is fine today, I will go on a picnic.
2 가정법 미래   If it should be true, I shall be happy.
3 가정법 과거   If I were rich, I would buy an airplane.
4 가정법 과거완료   If I had been rich, I would have bought it.

Pattern Practice

1. She got up early in the morning.

2. I didn't get up early yesterday.

3. Did you go to school by bus?

4. Where did you sleep the day before yesterday?

5. Do you go to school by bus or by car?

6. It is rainy today, isn't it?

7. Do you know when she will leave here?

8. How beautiful this flower is!

9. What a beautiful flower this is!

10. Open the window.

11. Don't open the window.

12. Let me go there.

13. Let me not go there.

14. Let her study hard.

15. Don't let her study hard.

16. Work hard, and you will succeed.

17. Work hard, or you will fail.

18. If I were a bird, I would fly to you.

19. If I had been a bird, I would have flown to you.

20. If it should rain today, I will not go to the party.

1. 다음 영문을 우리말로 옮기시오.

    (1) You had better not be late this morning. _____

    (2) Why were you late for school yesterday? _____

    (3) When do you get up in the morning? _____

    (4) I don't know when you get up in the morning. _____

    (5) You are ill, aren't you? _____

    (6) Did he stay at home yesterday? _____

    (7) How wonderful this city is! _____

    (8) Let's go to the party. _____

    (9) Let us go to the party. _____

    (10) Let her study English hard. _____

    (11) Study hard, and you will pass the examination. _____

    (12) Go home early, or you can not go home. _____

    (13) Don't go out too late at night. _____

    (14) Let her not go out by herself at night. _____

    (15) If you go to her birthday party, you will be happy. _____

2. 다음 문장을 영작하시오.

    (1) 당신은 지금 어디에 사십니까? _____

    (2) 당신은 그가 어디에 사는지 아십니까? _____

    (3) 이 자동차는 참 근사한데요! _____

    (4) 집에 일찍 갑시다. _____

    (5) 밤에 너무 늦게 외출하지 마라. _____

가정법의 종류

1. If it **rains** tomorrow, I **will** stay at home.	내일 비가 오면 나는 집에 머물 것이다.
2. If it **should** rain, I **will** stay at home all day.	혹시라도 내일 비가 오면 나는 하루 종일 집에 머물 것이다.
3. If I **were** a bird, I **would** fly to you.	만일 내가 새라면 너에게 날아갈 텐데.
4. If I **had been** a bird, I **would have flown** to you.	만일 내가 새였더라면 너에게 날아갔을 텐데.

1 가정법 현재 현재 또는 미래의 단순한 가정이나 불확실한 상상을 나타낸다.

조건절(종속절) 만일 ~한다면	귀결절(주절) ~할 것이다
If ~ 원형(현재형)	~ shall(will) + 원형

- If it **is**(be) fine tomorrow, I **will** go on a picnic.
- If he **calls**(call) this afternoon, tell him to wait.

2 가정법 미래 현재 또는 미래에 대한 강한 의심이나 거의 있을 수 없는 일을 상상하는 표현이다.

조건절(종속절) 만일 ~한다면	귀결절(주절) ~할 것이다

If ⌈ should ⌉ + 원형
  ⌊ were to ⌋
	~ ⌈ would(will) ⌉ + 원형
	  ⌊ should(shall) ⌋

1 조건절에 should를 쓰는 경우

미래에 대한 강한 의심을 나타낸다.
조건절에는 인칭에 관계없이 should를 쓴다.
귀결절에서 would(should)는 가정의 뜻이 강하고 will(shall)은 가정의 뜻이 약하다.

- If it **should** rain tomorrow, I **would** not start.
- If I **should** fail, I **will** try again.

가정법 현재와 가정법 미래의 차이
- 가정법 현재: 있을 수 있는 현재, 미래의 일을 가정한다.
- 가정법 미래: 거의 불가능한 미래를 가정한다.

2 **조건절에 were to를 쓰는 경우**   미래의 실현성 없는 상상을 나타낸다.

- If the sun **were to** rise in the west, I **would** marry you.
- If I **were to** be young again, I **would** be a poet.

3 가정법 과거   현재 사실의 반대를 가정하는 표현이다.

조건절(종속절) 만일 ~한다면	귀결절(주절) ~할 텐데
If ~ were (과거형)	~ ┌ would, should ┐ + 원형 └ could, might ┘

- If I **were** rich, I **could** buy a nice car.
  - = As I am not rich, I can not buy a nice car.
- If I **had** many friends, I **would** be very happy.
  - = As I don't have many friends, I am not very happy.
- If she **were** not happy, I **would** be unhappy.
  - = As she is happy, I am not unhappy.
- If you **didn't** study hard, you **would** not succeed.
  - = As you study hard, you will succeed.
- If I **had** a wing, I **could** fly to you.
  - = As I don't have a wing, I can not fly to you.

4 가정법 과거완료   과거 사실의 반대를 가정하는 표현이다.

- If I **had been** rich, I **could have bought** a nice car.
  - = As I was not rich, I could not buy a nice car.
- If I **had had** many friends, I **would have been** very happy.
  - = As I didn't have many friends, I was not very happy.
- If she **had** not **been** happy, I **would have been** unhappy.
  - = As she was happy, I was not unhappy.
- If you **had** not **studied** hard, you **would** not **have succeeded**.
  - = As you studied hard, you succeeded.
- If I **had had** a wing, I **could have flown** to you.
  - = As I didn't have a wing, I could not fly to you.

주의해야 할 가정법

P·r·e·v·i·e·w

1. **I wish I were** beautiful.
2. She looks **as if** she **were** ill.
3. **If it were not for** water, nothing **could** grow.
4. **Were** I a bird, I **would** fly to you.
5. **To hear** him speak English,
   you **would** take him for an American.

내가 아름답다면 좋을 텐데.
그녀는 아픈 것처럼 보인다.
물이 없다면 아무것도 자랄 수 없을 것이다.
만일 내가 새라면 너에게 날아갈 텐데.
그가 영어로 말하는 것을 들으면
당신은 그를 미국인으로 생각할 것이다.

---

1 I wish + 가정법 실현할 수 없는 소원을 나타낸다. (~하면 좋을 텐데)

1 I wish + 가정법 과거 현재의 이룰 수 없는 일을 소망하는 표현이다.

- **I wish I were** young.
  = I am sorry I am not young.
- **I wish I had** a good friend.
  = I am sorry I don't have a good friend.

2 I wish + 가정법 과거완료 과거에 이루지 못한 소망을 나타낸다.

- **I wish I had been** rich.
  = I am sorry I was not rich.
- **I wish I had had** a good friend.
  = I am sorry I didn't have a good friend.

2 as if + 가정법 현재와 과거의 사실에 반대되는 일을 가정하는 표현이다. (마치 ~처럼)

1 as if + 가정법 과거 마치 ~처럼

- He talks **as if** he **were** a professor.
- He talked **as if** he **were** a professor.
- She talks **as if** he **knew** everything.

2 as if + 가정법 과거완료 마치 ~했던 것처럼

- He talks **as if** he **had been** a professor.
- He talked **as if** he **had been** a professor.
- She talks **as if** he **had known** everything.

3 If it were not for ~ = But for ~ = Without ~ ~이 없다면

- **If it were not for** your help, I **might fail**.
  - = **But for** your help, I **might fail**.
  - = **Without** your help, I **might fail**.
- **If it were not for** the sun, we **could** not **live**.
  - = **But for** the sun, we **could** not **live**.
  - = **Without** the sun, we **could** not **live**.

4 If it had not been for ~ = But for ~ = Without ~ ~이 없었더라면

- **If it had not been for** your help, I **might have failed**.
  - = **But for** your help, I **might have failed**.
  - = **Without** your help, I **might have failed**.
- **If it had not been for** the sun, we **could** not **have lived**.
  - = **But for** the sun, we **could** not **have lived**.
  - = **Without** the sun, we **could** not **have lived**.

5 If를 생략할 경우   If를 생략하면 〈조동사, 동사 + 주어〉의 도치 구문이 된다.

- **Were I** a bird, I **would fly** to you.
- **Had I studied** English hard, I **would have passed** the exam.

6 부정사가 조건절을 대신하는 경우

- I should be happy **to meet** you again.
  - = If I meet you again, I should be happy.
- **To hear** her speak English, you would be surprised.
  - = If you heard her speak English, you would be surprised.

7 분사가 조건절을 대신하는 경우

- **Turning** to the right, you will find the building.
  - = If you turn to the right, you will find the building.
- **Born** in the country, she would never see such a tall building.
  - = If she were born in the country, she would never see such a tall building.

8 가정법 포함한 관용어구(If의 대용어구)

Suppose = if: 만일 ~하기만 한다면, in case = if: ~할 경우에는
unless = if ~ not: 만일 ~하지 않는다면, as it were: 말하자면, if ever: 설사 ~해도

Pattern Practice

1. If it **be** fine today, I **will** go out.

2. If it **should** rain tomorrow, I **will** not go to Mt. Seorak.

3. If she **were** rich, she **would** go to Paris.

4. If her father **had been** rich, she **could have studied** more.

5. I **wish** you **were** happy.

6. I **wish** you **had been** happy.

7. He talks **as if** he **knew** everything.

8. He talks **as if** he **had known** everything.

9. He talked **as if** he **knew** everything.

10. He talked **as if** he **had known** everything.

11. **If it were not for** water, we **could** not **live** any more.

12. **If it had not been for** water, we **could** not **have lived** any more.

13. **But for** the earth, where **could** we **live**?

14. **Without** you, I **would** not **have lived** any more.

15. **To see** her write a letter in English, you would be surprised.

16. **Being** tired, you had better go to bed early tonight.

17. **Unless** you study hard, you will fail in the examination.

18. **In case** I should fail, I would try again.

19. **Had you worked** hard, you **would have succeeded**.

20. A wise person **would** not **do** such a thing.

연습문제

1. 다음 영문을 우리말로 옮기시오.

   (1) If he were honest, I would like him. _____

   (2) If he had been honest, I would have liked him. _____

   (3) If I had much money, I could buy a nice car. _____

   (4) If I had had much money, I could have bought a nice car. _____

   _____

   (5) If it should rain tomorrow, I will not go to the meeting. _____

   _____

   (6) I wish I were young. _____

   (7) If I were to be a boy again, I would study very hard. _____

   (8) She talks as if she were a doctor. _____

   (9) Without your help, I would not succeed. _____

   (10) Unless you work hard, you will not succeed. _____

   (11) If it were not for water, nothing could live on the earth. _____

   _____

   (12) But for the sun, we could not have lived any more. _____

   _____

   (13) I wish I had known everything. _____

   (14) She talked as if she had known everything. _____

   (15) I should be happy to meet her again. _____

2. 다음 문장을 영작하시오.
   (1) 내가 부자라면 좋을 텐데. _____

   (2) 내가 새라면 당신에게 날아갈 텐데. _____

   (3) 그는 자기가 과학자인 것처럼 말한다. _____

   (4) 그녀가 가난했더라면 대학에 가지 못했을 텐데. _____

   (5) 아저씨의 도움이 없었더라면 나는 성공하지 못했을 텐데. _____

3. 다음 ( ) 안에서 알맞은 말을 고르시오.

(1) If I (was, were) a doctor, I could help you.

(2) If she had been rich, she would (buy, have bought) a nice house.

(3) If she were rich, she would (buy, have bought) a nice house.

(4) If it (shall, should) rain, I will not go out.

(5) If he (is, were) honest, I will meet him.

4. 다음 ( ) 안에 알맞은 말을 써 넣으시오.

(1) Study hard, ( ) you will succeed.

(2) Work hard, ( ) you will fail.

(3) I should be happy ( ) meet her again.

(4) ( ) wonderful the sky is!

(5) ( ) her go home quickly.

(6) If the sun ( ) to rise in the west, I would marry you.

(7) But ( ) your help, I would not succeed.

(8) He is, as it ( ), a real doctor for human being.

(9) If she ( ) had much money, she could have bought a nice car.

(10) It is natural that one ( ) obey the traffic laws.

5. 다음 두 문장의 뜻이 같아지도록 ( ) 안에 알맞을 말을 써 넣으시오.

(1) If it were not for water, nothing could live.

= ( ) ( ) water, nothing could live.

(2) If it had not been for your help, she could not have succeeded.

= ( ) your help, she could not have succeeded.

(3) If I knew his address, I could write a letter to him.

= ( ) I ( ) know his address, I ( ) write a letter to him.

(4) If I had known his address, I could have written him a letter.

= ( ) I ( ) know his address, I ( ) write him a letter.

(5) I wish I were young.

= I am sorry I ( ) ( ) young.

1. 다음 두 문장의 뜻이 같아지도록 밑줄 친 곳에 알맞은 말을 써 넣으시오.

(1) If I were rich, I could go to college.

= As _____

(2) If I had been rich, I could have studied more.

= As _____

(3) I wish I spoke English well.

= I _____

(4) I wish I had spoken English well.

= I _____

(5) But for the sun, we could not live.

= If _____

(6) Without the sun, we could not have lived.

= If _____

(7) If he had a beautiful girl friend, he would be happy.

= As _____

(8) If I had not had much money, I would not have bought a nice car.

= As _____

2. 다음 문장에서 잘못된 곳이 있으면 바르게 고치시오.

(1) I wish I was beautiful.

_____

(2) If I had enough money, I would have bought a nice house.

_____

(3) If it will rain tomorrow, I will not go on a picnic.

_____

(4) If he was a bird, he could fly to her.

_____

(5) Without for water, we could not live.

_____

(6) Work hard, or you will succeed.

_____

(7) If I had been a doctor, I would help her.

_____

Part 8

화법

NARRATION

1. He **is** a student.　　　　　　　　　그는 학생이다.
2. He and she **are** students.　　　　　그와 그녀는 학생이다.
3. She **says** that she **is** a teacher.　　그녀는 선생이라고 말한다.
4. She **said** that she **was** a teacher.　그녀는 선생이라고 말했다.
5. He **said** to me, "I **am** busy."　　그는 나에게 "나는 바쁘다."라고 말했다.
6. He **told** me that he **was** busy.　그는 자기가 바쁘다고 나에게 말했다.

직접화법을 간접화법으로 바꿀 때에는 수의 일치와 시제의 일치가 아주 중요하다.

1 수의 일치　　동사는 주어의 인칭과 수에 따라 동사의 꼴이 다르다. 이를 주어와 동사의 일치라고 한다.

2 시제의 일치　　복문에서 주절과 종속절의 시제는 서로 맞아야 한다. 이를 시제의 일치라고 한다.

3 화법　　다른 사람의 말을 전하는 방법을 화법이라고 한다. 화법에는 직접화법과 간접화법이 있다.

　1 직접화법　　남이 한 말을 그대로 전달하는 형식이다.

　　① 평서문의 화법
　　② 의문문의 화법 (의문사가 없는)
　　③ 의문문의 화법 (의문사가 있는)
　　④ 명령문의 화법
　　⑤ 감탄문의 화법

　2 간접화법　　남이 한 말을 내용만 전달하는 형식이다.

1. She and I **are** happy.
2. She or I **am** happy.
3. Either you or he **is** wrong.
4. Ten years **is** a long time.

그녀와 나는 행복하다.
그녀나 나는 행복하다.
당신과 그 사람 중에서 한 사람은 나쁘다.
10년은 긴 세월이다.

동사는 주어의 인칭과 수에 따라서 동사의 꼴이 다르다. 이를 주어와 동사의 수의 일치라고 한다.

1 주어가 and로 결합되면 동사는 복수동사로 받는다.

· He **and** I **are** good friends.
= We are good friends.
· The boy **and** the girl **were** running over there.
= They were running over there.

▶▶ 주어가 비록 and로 결합되지만 복수동사로 받지 않을 때도 있다.

· Bread **and** butter **is** my favorite food.
· Romeo **and** Juliet **was** written by Shakespeare.
· A black **and** white dog **is** running over there.
cf. A black **and** a white dog **are** running over there.

2 주어가 or로 결합되면 or 뒤의 주어에 일치한다.

· Either she **or** I **am** good.
· Neither you **or** he **is** wrong.

3 every는 여러 개가 있어도 단수 취급을 한다.

· **Every** boy **and every** girl **is** singing.
· **Each** boy **and each** girl **has** a desk.

4 복수형 주어가 단수 동사를 취할 때   시간, 거리, 가격, 무게를 나타내는 명사는 단수 취급한다.

· Ten **years is** a long time for you.
· Ten **miles is** a long distance.
cf. **Mathematics** is difficult.

Chapter 02

시제의 일치

1. He **says** that he **is** honest.	그는 정직하다고 말한다.
2. He **said** that he **was** honest.	그는 정직하다고 말했다.
3. She **thinks** that she **was** happy.	그녀는 행복했다고 생각한다.
4. She **thought** that she **had been** happy.	그녀는 행복했다고 생각했다.

복문에서 주절의 동사와 종속절의 동사는 그 시제가 서로 맞아야 한다. 이를 시제의 일치라고 한다.

1 주절의 동사가 현재(미래, 현재완료)이면 종속절의 시제는 제한이 없다.

- I (will) **think** that
  - she **is** happy.
  - she **was** happy.
  - she **will be** happy.
  - she **has been** happy.

2 주절의 동사가 과거일 때 종속절의 동사는, 현재의 경우 과거가 된다.

- I **think** that he is right.
- I **thought** that he **was** right.

- He **says** that he **is** a teacher.
- He **said** that he **was** a teacher.

- She **says** that she **will study** hard.
- She **said** that she **would study** hard.

3 주절의 동사가 과거이면 종속절의 동사는 과거와 현재완료의 경우, 과거완료가 되어야 한다.

- I **think** that she **was** right.
- I **thought** that she **had been** right.

- He **says** that he **has been** ill.
- He **said** that he **had been** ill.

시제 일치의 예외

❶ 불변의 진리는 항상 현재형을 쓴다.
- He **said** that the sun is larger than the earth.
- He **thought** that the earth is round.

❷ 현재의 습관과 사실은 현재형을 쓴다.

  · He **said** that he **gets** up early every morning.
  · He **said** that the first train **leaves** at six in the morning.

❸ 역사적인 사실은 항상 과거로 쓴다.

  · She **said** that Columbus **discovered** America in 1492. (○)
  · She **said** that Columbus **had discovered** America in 1492. (×)

❹ 가정법의 시제는 변하지 않는다.

  · She **says** that she **would** be happy if she were young.
  · She **said** that she **would** be happy if she were young.

  · He **speaks** English as if he **were** an American.
  · He **spoke** English as if he **were** an American.

❺ 비교를 나타낼 때는 시제의 제한이 없다.

  · She **is** more beautiful than she **was**.
  · It **was** warmer yesterday than it **is** today.

직접화법을 간접화법으로 바꿀 때 주의할 점

❶ 지시대명사, 장소와 때의 부사, 형용사 등은 전달 동사가 과거이면 다음과 같이 바뀐다.

this → that	yesterday → the day before
these → those	the previous day
here → there	tomorrow → the next day
now → then	the following day
today → that day	last night → the night before
ago → before	next week → the next week

❷ 인칭대명사의 변화 (피전달문" "안의 인칭대명사)

  ⓐ 1인칭(I, my, me, we, our, us): 전달문의 주어와 일치한다.
  ⓑ 2인칭(you, your): 전달문의 목적어와 일치한다.
  ⓒ 3인칭(he, his, him, she, her): 그대로 한다.

Pattern Practice

1. He **and** I **are** good students.

2. He **or** I **am** a good student.

3. Either you **or** I **am** right.

4. Neither he **nor** you **are** right.

5. Curry **and** rice is my favorite food.

6. **Not only** she **but also** I **am** beautiful.

7. I **as well as** she **am** beautiful.

8. My family **is** a large one.

9. My family **are** all busy.

10. **Every** man **and every** woman **is** working hard.

11. Ten years **is** a long time.

12. He **thinks** that I **am** diligent.

13. He **thinks** that I **was** diligent.

14. He **thinks** that I **will be** diligent.

15. He **thinks** that I **have been** diligent.

16. She **thought** that I **was** honest.

17. She **thought** that I **had been** honest.

18. She **thought** that the earth **is** round.

19. She **thought** that I **go** to the park every morning.

20. He **thinks** that the late President Lincoln **was** a great man.

연습문제

1. 다음 영문을 우리말로 옮기시오.

(1) Either he or you are wrong. _____

(2) Neither he nor I am wrong. _____

(3) Romeo and Juliet is a famous play written by Shakespeare. _____

_____

(4) I can speak not only English but also French. _____

(5) I can speak French as well as English. _____

(6) My class is a large one. _____

(7) My class are all diligent. _____

(8) Every boy and every girl is learning English. _____

(9) Each boy and each girl has a desk. _____

(10) Mathematics is difficult for us to study. _____

(11) She believes that I am honest. _____

(12) She believed that I was honest. _____

(13) He believed that the sun is larger than the moon. _____

(14) Do you know who invented the radio? _____

(15) He said that she goes for a walk every morning. _____

2. 다음 문장을 영작하시오.

(1) 나의 가족은 모두가 바쁘다. _____

(2) 너와 나 중에서 하나는 나쁘다. _____

(3) 그는 그녀가 정직하다고 생각한다. _____

(4) 그는 그녀가 정직하다고 생각했다. _____

(5) 당신뿐 아니라 그도 잘생겼다. _____

화법

1 평서문의 화법

P · r · e · v · i · e · w

1. He **says**, "I **am** busy."　　　　　　　　　그는 "나는 바쁘다."라고 말한다.
    He **says** that he **is** busy.　　　　　　　그는 자기가 바쁘다고 말한다.
2. He **said to** me, "I **am** busy."　　　　　그는 나에게 "나는 바쁘다."라고 말했다.
    He **told** me that he **was** busy.　　　　그는 자기가 바쁘다고 나에게 말했다.

평서문의 간접화법을 만드는 방법

❶ say(said) → say(said) 그대로 쓰고,
　　say(said) to → tell(told)로 바꾸어 쓴다.
❷ 콤마(,)와 인용부호("")를 없앤다.
❸ 접속사 that을 쓴다. (생략해도 좋다.)
❹ 피전달문의 인칭대명사는 전달자의 입장에서 바꾼다.
❺ 시제를 일치시킨다.
❻ 지시대명사, 형용사, 부사 등을 전달하는 입장에 맞도록 고친다.

· She **says**, "**I am** happy."
　　She **says** that **she is** happy.

· She **said**, "**I am** happy now."
　　She **said** that **she was** happy **then**.

· He **said to** me, "I **know** you."
　　He **told** me that he **knew** me.

· He **said to** me, "I **gave** her **this** book **yesterday**."
　　He **told me** that he **had given** her **that** book **the day before**.

· You **said to her**, "You **will** get well **tomorrow**."
　　You **told her** that she **would** get well **the next day**.

· He **said**, "I **will** do it **here**."
　　He **said** that he **would** do it **there**.

2 의문문의 화법

1. She **said to** me, "**What** do you want?"
   She **asked** me **what** I wanted.
2. She **said to** me, "**Did** you want a book?"
   She **asked** me **if** I **had wanted** a book.

그녀는 나에게 내가 무엇을 원하느냐고 물었다.

그녀는 나에게 내가 책을 원했는지 물었다.

의문문의 간접화법을 만드는 방법

❶ said to → asked로 바꾸어 쓴다.
❷ 콤마(,)와 인용부호("")를 없앤다.
❸ 의문사가 있으면 그대로 쓴다.
❹ 의문사가 없으면 접속사 if나 whether를 쓴다.
❺ 피전달문의 인칭대명사는 전달자의 입장에서 바꾼다.
❻ 지시대명사, 부사, 형용사 등을 전달하는 입장에 맞도록 고친다.

1 의문사가 없는 의문문의 화법

· He **said to** me, "**Are** you happy?"
  He **asked** me if I **was** happy.

· She **said to** him, "**Can** you speak Korean?"
  She **asked** him if he **could** speak Korean.

· She **said to** him, "**Does** he go to school?"
  She **asked** him **if** he **went** to school.

· He **said to** me, "**Will** you meet her?"
  He **asked** me **whether** I **would** meet her (or not).

2 의문사가 있는 의문문의 화법

· She **said to** me, "**Who** broke the window?"
  She **asked** me **who** had broken the window.

· He **said to** me, "**Where** do you live?"
  He **asked** me **where** I lived.

· He **said to** me, "**What** did she buy **yesterday**?"
  He **asked** me **what** she had bought **the day before**.

▶▶ 의문사와 접속사 if(whether)가 이끄는 절은 명사절로 간접의문문이다.

Pattern Practice

1. She **says**, "I **go** to school."

2. She **says**, "I **went** to school."

3. She **said**, "I **go** to school **today**."

4. She **said**, "I **went** to school **yesterday**."

5. He **said to me**, "I **gave** you this book **two days ago**."

6. He **said to me**, "I **send** her some flowers."

7. He **said to me**, "I **will write** a letter to you **next week**."

8. He **said to me**, "**Do** you like her?"

9. He **said to me**, "**Did** you like me?"

10. She **said to me**, "**Who** broke the window?"

11. She **said to me**, "**When** do you meet her?"

12. She **said to me**, "**Where** did you meet me **last month**?"

13. He **said to me**, "**Why** were you absent from school **yesterday**?"

14. He **said to me**, "**Will** you give me a book **tomorrow**?"

15. He **said to me**, "**Are** you **reading** a book **now**?"

16. He **said to me**, "**Were** you late for school **yesterday**?"

17. He **said to her**, "**Is** she **writing** a letter?"

18. She **said to her**, "**Do** you read this book here?"

19. She **said to her**, "**Did** you make me happy?"

20. She **said to her**, "**Can** you help me to cook lunch now?"

3 명령문의 화법

1. I **said to** him, "Study English hard."
   I **told** him **to** study English hard.
2. She **said to** me, "Please don't open the door."
   She **asked** me **not to** open the door.
3. He **said to** us, "**Let's** go to the mountain."
   He **suggested** that we should go to the mountain.

나는 그에게 영어를 열심히 공부하라고 말했다.

그녀는 나에게 문을 열지 말라고 부탁했다.

그는 우리에게 산에 가자고 제안했다.

명령문의 간접화법을 만드는 방법

❶ said to → told(asked, ordered, advised) 등으로 바꾸어 쓴다.
❷ 피전달문의 동사는 to부정사로 고친다.
❸ 부정명령문의 동사는 not to부정사로 고친다.
❹ 피전달문의 인칭대명사는 전달자의 입장에서 바꾼다.
❺ 지시대명사, 부사, 형용사 등을 전달하는 입장에 맞도록 고친다.
❻ Let's로 시작되는 제안 명령문의 화법은 said to를 suggested, proposed로 바꾸고 that 명사절에는 should를 쓴다.

· She **said to** me, "Go home quickly."
  She **told** me **to go** home quickly.

· She **said to** me, "Don't go home quickly."
  She **told me not to go** home quickly.

· She **said to** me, "Please go home quickly."
  She **asked** me **to go** home quickly.

· The doctor **said to** me, "Don't smoke too much."
  The doctor **advised** me not to smoke too much.

· The officer **said to** him, "Don't be late for the meeting."
  The officer **ordered** him not to be late for the meeting.

· He **said to** us, "Let's read books."
  He **proposed** that we should read books.

4 감탄문의 화법 및 그 밖의 화법

P · r · e · v · i · e · w

1. He **said**, "How beautiful she **is**!"
   He **cried** out **how** beautiful she **was**.
   He **said that** she **was very** beautiful.

   그는 그녀가 아름답다고 소리쳤다.

2. He **said**, "It **is** raining, **but** I **will** go out."
   He **said that** it **was** raining **but that** he **would** go out.

   그는 비가 오지만 외출할 것이라고 말했다.

감탄문의 간접화법을 만드는 방법

❶ said → cried out, exclaimed, shouted 등으로 (의문사 그대로의 경우)
   said → said로 (감탄문을 평서문으로 고친 후의 경우) 바꾸어 쓴다.
❷ 콤마(,)와 인용부호("")를 없앤다.
❸ 감탄문을 그대로 쓸 때에는 의문사를 접속사로 쓰고, 감탄문을 평서문으로 바꾸어 쓸 때에는 평서문의
   화법처럼 that을 쓴다.
❹ 피전달문의 인칭대명사는 전달자의 입장에서 바꾼다.
❺ 지시대명사, 부사, 형용사 등을 전달하는 입장에 맞도록 고친다.

· She **said**, "What a beautiful city Seoul is!"
  She **exclaimed what** a beautiful city Seoul **was**.
  She **said that** Seoul **was** a **very** beautiful city.

· He **said**, "How beautiful this flower is!"
  He **cried out how** beautiful **that** flower **was**.
  He **said that** flower **was very** beautiful.

· She **said**, "God bless you!"
  She **prayed that** God **might** bless me.

· He **said**, "Hurrah! we've won."
  He **shouted** with joy **that** they had won.

중문의 화법을 만드는 방법

〈평서문 + 평서문〉의 경우 and, but 뒤에 that을 쓰고 평서문, 명령문, 의문문 등이 섞일 때는 and로 연
결하되 각 화법을 전환하여 연결한다.

· He **said**, "I **am** busy now, but I **shall** be free tomorrow."
  He **said that** he **was** busy **then**, **but that** he would be free **the next day**.

· She **said to** me, "I like this book. Will you lend it to me?"
  She **told me that** she liked **that** book **and asked me if** I would lend it to her.

1. He said to me, "Go home now."

2. He said to me, "Don't go home now."

3. He said to me, "Please go home quickly."

4. He said to me, "Please don't go home quickly."

5. She said to me, "Don't smoke too much."

6. She said, "Let's go home."

7. She said, "Let's not go home."

8. The officer said to him, "Don't be late for the meeting."

9. He said, "How wonderful this house is!"

10. He said, "What a wonderful house this is!"

11. He said, "God bless you!"

12. She said, "How beautiful I am!"

13. She said, "What a beautiful lady I am!"

14. He said to me, "I am rich, but you are poor."

15. He said, "I don't like this blouse. Please show me another."

16. He said, "This is not a window. What is it?"

17. She told me that she would begin to learn English the next day.

18. She asked me if I had been late for school the day before.

19. She asked me where I bought that car.

20. She told me not to paly baseball in the park.

1. 다음 영문을 우리말로 옮기시오.

(1) She said, "I am happy." _____

(2) She said that she was happy. _____

(3) He said to me, "I like you." _____

(4) He told me that he liked me. _____

(5) He said to me, "I gave her this book yesterday." _____

(6) He told me that he had given her that book the day before. _____

_____

(7) She said to me, "Are you reading a book?" _____

(8) She asked me if I was reading a book. _____

(9) He said to me, "Were you absent from school two weeks ago?" _____

_____

(10) He asked me if I had been absent from school two weeks before. _____

_____

(11) She said to me, "What do you want?" _____

(12) She asked to me what I wanted. _____

(13) He said to me, "Go to school quickly." _____

(14) He told me to go to school quickly. _____

(15) She said, "How wonderful Seoul is!" _____

(16) She cried out how wonderful Seoul was. _____

2. 다음 문장을 영작하시오.

(1) 그녀는 나에게 영어를 열심히 공부하라고 말했다. _____

(2) 그녀는 나에게 어디에서 사느냐고 물었다. _____

(3) 그는 나에게 그녀가 무엇을 하고 있느냐고 물었다. _____

(4) 그는 나에게 집에 늦게 가지 말라고 말했다. _____

3. 다음 (   ) 안에서 알맞은 말을 고르시오.

   (1) He and I (are, am, is) happy.

   (2) He or I (are, am, is) happy.

   (3) Not only she but also I (are, am, is) working hard.

   (4) She as well as I (are, am, is) working hard.

   (5) Either he or I (are, am, is) wrong.

   (6) Neither he nor I (are, am, is) right.

   (7) My family (are, is) a large one.

   (8) My family (are, is) all busy.

   (9) Every boy and every girl (are, is) studying English hard.

   (10) Each man and each woman (have, has) a racket.

   (11) Bread and butter (are, is) my favorite food for breakfast.

   (12) Romeo and Juliet (were, was) written by Shakespeare.

   (13) Mathematics (are, is) difficult for the students.

   (14) Twenty years (are, is) a long time to wait.

   (15) She said that she (is, was) honest.

   (16) She said that she (is, had been) honest.

   (17) He said that the sun (is, was) round.

   (18) She said that she (goes, went) to the park every morning.

   (19) She says that Columbus (discovers, discovered) America in 1492.

   (20) He (said, asked) if he would stay at home.

   (21) She is more beautiful than she (is, was).

   (22) He cried out (how, that) beautiful the flower was.

   (23) He said (how, that) the flower was very beautiful.

4. 다음 두 문장의 뜻이 같아지도록 (   ) 안에 알맞은 말을 써 넣으시오.

   (1) He said, "I am happy now."

      He said that he (   ) happy (   ).

   (2) She said to me, "I gave you too much money."

      She told me that she (   ) (   ) me too much money.

(3) She said to me, "I will leave here tomorrow."

She told me that she (　　) leave (　　) (　　) (　　) (　　).

(4) He said to me, "Are you writing a letter?"

He asked me (　　) (　　) was writing a letter.

(5) He said to me, "What do you want to do?"

He asked me (　　) (　　) wanted to do.

(6) She said to me, "Who broke the window?"

She asked me (　　) (　　) broken the window.

(7) He said to me, "Go home quickly."

He told me (　　) go home quickly.

(8) She said, "Let's go out quickly."

She (　　　　　) (　　　　) we should go out quickly.

(9) He said, "How pretty the girl is!"

He (　　) (　　) (　　) pretty the girl was.

(10) He said, "What a pretty girl she is!"

He (　　) (　　) she was a very pretty girl.

5. 다음 문장에서 잘못된 곳이 있으면 바르게 고치시오.

(1) She said that she takes a bath every week. _____

(2) He told me that he saw my sister the day before. _____

_____

(3) I thought that he is very weak. _____

(4) She told me to not smoke again. _____

(5) I didn't believe that she studies hard. _____

(6) He asked me when did I study. _____

(7) She cried out how cold it is. _____

(8) He told me that Columbus had discovered America. _____

_____

1. 다음 문장을 간접화법으로 고치시오.

   (1) She said, "I am very happy here." _____

   (2) She said to me, "I gave you this book yesterday." _____

   _____

   (3) He said to me, "Are you busy now?" _____

   (4) He said to me, "Is he reading a book?" _____

   (5) She said to me, "What do you want to do?" _____

   (6) She said to me, "Who invented the radio?" _____

   (7) He said to me, "Where did she buy the car last week?" _____

   _____

   (8) He said to me, "Study English hard." _____

   (9) She said to me, "Don't be late tonight." _____

   (10) She said to me, "Please close the door." _____

   (11) He said, "Let's have lunch at twelve." _____

   (12) He said, "How tall this building is!" _____

   (13) She said, "God bless you." _____

   (14) He said, "She is very kind. I want to meet her." _____

   (15) The doctor said to me, "Don't smoke too much for your health." _____

   _____

2. 다음 문장을 직접화법으로 고치시오.

   (1) He told me that he had been a pilot. _____

   (2) She told me to be kind to others. _____

   (3) He asked me if I would get up early in the morning. _____

   _____

   (4) She asked me when I had bought that car. _____

   _____

   (5) He said that he was happy then. _____

Part 9

접속사

CONJUNCTION

1. He **and** I are good friends.   그와 나는 좋은 친구이다.
2. I think **that** he is honest.   나는 그가 정직하다고 생각한다.
3. **Not only** she **but also** I am busy.   그녀뿐만 아니라 나도 바쁘다.

낱말과 낱말, 구와 구, 절과 절을 연결시키는 구실을 하는 것을 접속사라고 한다.

1 형태상의 분류

1 단순 접속사 한 개의 낱말로 된 접속사

and, but, or, that, when, if 등

- He is diligent, **but** she is idle.
- I don't know **when** she will arrive here.

2 구 접속사 두 낱말 이상이 하나의 접속사 구실을 하는 것

as soon as, as if 등

- **As soon as** she saw me, he ran away.
- He talks **as if** he were a president.

3 상관 접속사

either ~ or, not only ~ but also 등

- **Either** he **or** I am wrong.
- I can speak **not only** English **but also** French.

2 기능상의 분류

1 등위 접속사

2 종속 접속사

① 명사절
② 형용사절
③ 부사절

Chapter 01 등위접속사

P·r·e·v·i·e·w

1. He is honest **and** diligent.	그는 정직하고 부지런하다.
2. He is not honest, **but** diligent.	그는 정직하지 않지만 부지런하다.
3. Is he honest **or** dishonest?	그는 정직합니까, 아니면 부정직합니까?
4. **Both** Mary **and** Jack are honest.	메리와 잭은 정직하다.

낱말과 낱말, 구와 구, 절과 절을 문법상 대등한 관계로 연결시켜 주는 접속사를 등위접속사라고 한다.
등위 접속사에는 and, but, or, so, for, both ~ and, not only ~ but also, as well as, either ~ or,
neither ~ nor 등이 있다.

1 and의 용법

- Mary **and** Tom are happy.
- Mary, Tom, **and** Jack are happy.
- Mary is happy, **and** Tom is not happy.
- Tom is good, **and** diligent.
- Study hard, **and** you will succeed.
    = If you study hard, you will succeed.
- Come **and** see me.
    = Come **to** see me.
    ▶▶ 〈come, go, try + and + 동사원형〉의 형태에서 and는 to의 대용으로 쓰인다.

2 but의 용법

- He can speak English, **but** can not speak Japanese.
- He can speak English, **but** she can not speak English.
- She is **not** a teacher, **but** a doctor.

3 or의 용법

- Do you like an apple **or** an orange?
- The distance is a mile **or** about 1.7 kilometers.
- Study hard, **or** you will fail.
    = If you don't study hard, you will fail.

Part 9 접속사 Conjunction

4 for의 용법

· I didn't do my homework, **for** I was sick.
· I couldn't go to the party, **for** it was raining all day.

▶▶ for가 접속사로 쓰일 때는 앞에 콤마(,)가 온다. 뜻은 '왜냐하면 ~이기 때문이다'이다.

5 so의 용법

· I was sick, **so** I was late for school.
   = **As** I was sick, I was late for school.

▶▶ '그래서'라는 뜻으로 결과나 결론을 나타낸다.

6 both ~ and의 용법

· **Both** she **and** I are good friends.
· I like **both** pop music **and** classical music.

▶▶ both A and B: A와 B 둘 다

7 not only ~ but (also)와 as well as의 용법

· **Not only** you **but also** I am right.
· I **as well as** you am right.

▶▶ not only A but also B: A뿐만 아니라 B도 역시 (동사는 B에 일치)
   B as well as A: A는 물론 B도 역시 (동사는 B에 일치)

8 either ~ or의 용법

· **Either** you **or** he is wrong.
· **We** must learn **either** French **or** German.

▶▶ either A or B: A나 B 중 어느 하나 (양자택일)

9 neither ~ nor의 용법

· **Neither** you **nor** he is wrong.
· We can speak **neither** English nor French.

▶▶ neither A nor B: A도 B도 ~아니다 (양자 부정)

· I like **neither** coffee **nor** milk.
   = I don't like **either** coffee **or** milk.

1. She **and** I are good friends.

2. You, she and I **are** good friends.

3. He **or** I am a good student.

4. He is old, **but** strong.

5. He is **not** idle, **but** diligent.

6. Which do you like better, spring **or** summer?

7. Which do you like best, spring, summer, **or** winter?

8. Please go **and** have lunch.

9. Go home quickly, **and** you will see her.

10. Go home quickly, **or** you will not see her.

11. He was late this morning, **for** he got up too late.

12. I can speak **not only** English **but also** French.

13. I can speak French **as well as** English.

14. **Either** she **or** I am busy.

15. **Neither** she **nor** I am busy.

16. **Both** she **and** I are busy.

17. I was too tired, **so** I went to bed early.

18. **As** I was too tired, I went to bed early.

19. Come **and** see me in the morning.

20. I like **neither** coffee **nor** milk.

연습문제

1. 다음 영문을 우리말로 옮기시오.

(1) Tom and Jack are brothers. _____

(2) Tom, Jack, and Benjamin are my classmates. _____

(3) Which do you like better, coffee or milk? _____

(4) Come and see me right now. _____

(5) Try to do, and you will do anything. _____

(6) Make a friend, or you will be unhappy. _____

(7) I caught cold last night, for I slept in the cold room. _____

_____

(8) Not only he but also you are a good teacher. _____

(9) You as well as he are a good teacher. _____

(10) I like both Tom and Mary. _____

(11) Either she or I am happy. _____

(12) Neither she nor I am happy. _____

(13) As I am busy, I cannot go to your birthday party. _____

_____

(14) I was busy, so I could not go to your birthday party. _____

_____

(15) She doesn't like either summer or winter. _____

2. 다음 문장을 영작하시오.

(1) 열심히 일하라, 그러면 당신은 성공할 것이다. _____

(2) 좋은 사람이 되라, 그렇지 않으면 그들은 당신을 좋아하지 않을 것이다. _____

_____

(3) 오늘 저녁에 저를 보러 오십시오. _____

(4) 나는 일본어뿐만 아니라 중국어도 말할 수 있다. _____

(5) 톰과 잭 어느 쪽도 나쁘지 않다. _____

1. I think **that** she can speak English.
2. I know the man **who** teaches us English.
3. I will leave here **when** he arrives here.

나는 그녀가 영어를 말할 수 있다고 생각한다.
나는 우리에게 영어를 가르치는 분을 안다.
그가 여기에 도착할 때 나는 여기를 떠나겠다.

종속절을 이끄는 접속사를 종속접속사라고 한다. 종속접속사에는 명사절, 형용사절, 부사절을 이끄는 접속사가 있다.

1 명사절을 이끄는 종속접속사

1 that의 용법 that이 이끄는 명사절은 주어, 목적어, 보어 역할을 한다.

· That she will arrive here is certain. [주어]

= It is certain that she will arrive here.

▶▶ that절이 주어가 될 때에는 보통 that절을 It(가주어)으로 바꿔 놓고 that절(진주어)은 뒤에 놓는다.

· I know (that) he was an actor. [목적어]

▶▶ that절이 동사의 목적어가 될 때에는 that을 생략할 수 있다.

· My hope is that I become a scientist. [보어]

2 whether, if의 용법

· **Whether** she will come (or not) is doubtful. [주어]

= **It** is doubtful **whether** she will come (or not).

▶▶ It은 가주어, whether는 진주어이다. whether는 or not을 동반하는 경우가 종종 있다.

· I don't know **whether** he will come (or not). [목적어]
· I don't know **if** he will come. [목적어]

▶▶ if는 타동사의 목적어로만 이끌 수 있다.

· The question is **whether** he will come (or not). [보어]

cf. I don't know **what** he said. [목적어]

▶▶ 관계대명사 what도 명사절을 이끈다.

2 형용사절을 이끄는 종속접속사

1 관계대명사

· This is the person **who** teaches us English.
· This is the house **which** he lives in.

- This is the first Korean **that** flew across the Pacific.
  - *cf.* 동격의 that절: that절이 명사 뒤에 와서 그 명사와 동격을 이룰 때가 있다. '~라고 하는'의 뜻이 있다.
- I don't know the fact **that** she was rich.
- She has no hope **that** she will have much money.

2 관계부사

- This is the house **where** he lives.
- This is the place **where** the dog was killed. [형용사절]
- This is **where** the dog was killed. [명사절]

3 부사절을 이끄는 종속접속사

1 때를 나타내는 접속사　when, while, as, before, after, since, till, as soon as, as long as, whenever

- **When** I arrived here, the bus had left here.
- **While** I was walking along the street, I met him.
- **As** she was young, she lived in Busan.
- You had better brush your teeth **before** you go to bed.
- I studied hard **after** I had dinner.
- She has lived in Seoul **since** she was born.
- I will wait for you here **till** you come back.
- **As soon as** he saw a police officer, he ran away.
- I love you **as long as** I live.
- **Whenever** my father came home, he bought me some cake.

2 장소를 나타내는 접속사　where, wherever

- **Where** there is a will, there is a way.
- He was welcomed **wherever** he went.

3 원인, 이유를 나타내는 접속사　as, because, since

- **As** she was too tired, she went to bed early.
- You must stay at home **because** you are sick.
- **Since** I have no money, I cannot go to the beach.
- **Now** (**that**) he is busy, he can not come here early.
- She was absent from school, **for** she was sick.

TIP

because가 뜻이 가장 강하고 since, as, for 순으로 뜻은 '~때문에'이다.

❶ because, since, as, for의 문장 중의 위치

ⓐ because: 문장 앞에 오는 일이 드물다.

ⓑ as, since: 문장 앞에 오는 것이 보통이다.

ⓒ for: 문장 뒤에 온다.

❷ because와 for의 뜻

ⓐ because: 처음부터 생각하고 있는 원인

ⓑ for: 뒤에 생각난 이유 또는 첨가된 설명

4 **조건을 나타내는 접속사**   if, unless, so long as, in case 등

· **If** you are busy, you may stay at home.

· **Unless** you are busy, you may stay at home.

  = If you are not busy, you may stay at home.

· You may stay at home **so long as** you are sick.

· **In case** he comes, you may go out.

  ▶▶ 조건절에서는 미래 시제 대신에 현재 시제를 쓴다.

5 **양보를 나타내는 접속사**   though, although, even if, even though, as 등

· **Though**(**Although**) I live near his house, I don't know him.

· **Even if**(**though**) she is old, she can walk for a long time.

· Young **as** he is, he has much experience.

6 **목적을 나타내는 접속사**   that(so that, in order that) ~ may, lest(for fear that) ~ should

· I work hard (**so**) **that** I **may** succeed.

· I got up early **in order that** I **might** catch the first bus.

· I work hard **lest** I **should** fail in the examination.

· I got up early **for fear that** I **should** be late for school.

7 **결과를 나타내는 접속사**   ⟨so + (형용사, 부사) + that⟩, ⟨such + 명사 + that⟩, so that

· He is **so** old **that** he cannot go to mountain alone.

· She is **such** a good person **that** she is loved by everyone.

· He is old, **so that** he cannot go to the mountain alone.

  ▶▶ so that ~ may: 목적을 나타낸다.

      so that: 결과를 나타낸다.

8 비교, 정도를 나타내는 접속사   than, as, as ~ as, not so ~ as, as if, as though, as far as, so far as

- She is older **than** I.
- Do **as** you want to do.
- She is **as** beautiful **as** my mother.
- She is **not so** beautiful **as** my mother.
- He talks **as if** he were a president.
- He acts **as though** he were a soccer player.
- I went **as far as** Chuncheon.
- I walked **as far as** ten miles.
- **So far as** I am concerned, I have nothing to tell you.

9 그 밖의 접속사   no sooner ~ than/scarcely ~ when/hardly ~ before = as soon as, ever ~ may = no matter ~ may

- **No sooner** had I entered the room **than** they stood up.
  = **Scarcely** had I entered the room **when** they stood up.
  = **Hardly** had I entered the room **before** they stood up.
  = **As soon as** I entered the room, they stood up.

- **Whatever** you **may** say, I can not believe you.

- **However** hard you **may** try, you cannot finish the work.
  = **No matter how** hard you **may** try, you cannot finish the work.

- **However** rich you **may** be, you should not waste money.
  = **No matter how** rich you **may** be, you should not waste money.

1. **It** is certain **that** she will be a poet.

2. I thought **that** he was a great man in American history.

3. My plan is **that** I become a pianist.

4. I don't know **whether** she will come soon.

5. Can you tell me **if** he will build the building?

6. I will go for a walk **if** it is fine tomorrow.

7. Can you understand **what** he said?

8. This is the best book **that** was written by Mr. Bang.

9. This is the place **where** she was born.

10. This is **where** she was born.

11. The fact **that** Admiral Yi Sunsin invented the turtle ship is great in the world history.

12. The book **that** I am looking for is in the National Library.

13. **When** I met him, he was very young and handsome.

14. **As** I was a boy, I lived in Busan.

15. **As** I was a boy, I could not go on a trip by myself.

16. My sister cannot go to college **because** she is ill.

17. I could not catch the first train, **for** I got up late this morning.

18. **As** she is busy, she cannot go to the meeting.

19. **Since** I am not strong, I cannot work for a long time.

20. You will be welcomed **wherever** you may go.

1. 다음 영문을 우리말로 옮기시오.

(1) I lost the same watch that my father had given me on my birthday. _____

_____

(2) I know the fact that he was a great musician. _____

(3) I thought that she was a famous poet. _____

(4) It is certain that she is a scientist. _____

(5) This is the same car that I bought the other day. _____

(6) Tell me what you want to do. _____

(7) Can you tell me whatever you want to have? _____

(8) I cannot remember the place where I met her at first. _____

_____

(9) Please tell me where you were born. _____

(10) While I was reading a newspaper, my brother watched TV.

_____

(11) As I was busy, I couldn't attend the meeting. _____

(12) Since he is tired, he wants to take a rest. _____

(13) He is missing her wherever she goes. _____

(14) She put on an overcoat, for it was too cold. _____

(15) We made a fire because it was cold. _____

2. 다음 문장을 영작하시오.

(1) 내가 어렸을 때 나는 공부를 열심히 했다. _____

(2) 당신이 어디를 가든 간에 당신은 나를 잊지 못할 것이다. _____

_____

(3) 내일 날씨가 좋다면 나는 여기에 머물 것이다. _____

(4) 나는 그가 가지고 있는 것을 가지고 싶다. _____

(5) 그녀는 피곤하므로 잠자리에 들기를 원한다. _____

Pattern Practice

1. **If** you meet me, you will be glad.

2. **Unless** you are honest, you will not be loved by her.

3. **Although** he is poor, he helps many friends.

4. Old **as** he is, he can make many things a day.

5. She works hard **so that** she may help her old mother.

6. He got up early **for fear that** he **should** miss the train.

7. We should work hard **lest** we **should** be behind the times.

8. The man is so weak **that** he **cannot** lift the box.

9. The man is **such** a weak man **that** he **cannot** lift the box.

10. The man is weak, **so that** he cannot lift the box.

11. She is more beautiful **than** my sister.

12. She is **as** beautiful **as** my sister.

13. She is **not so** beautiful **as** my sister.

14. He talked **as if** he were a lawyer.

15. He went **as far as** Busan.

16. That is not true, **so far as** I know.

17. **No sooner** had he finished school **than** he went abroad.

18. **As soon as** he finished school, he went abroad.

19. **However** hard you may try, you cannot finish the work.

20. **Whatever** you **may** say, he cannot believe you.

연습문제

1. 다음 영문을 우리말로 옮기시오.

(1) Unless you are diligent, you will not succeed. _____

(2) Though he is weak, he studies hard everyday. _____

(3) Young as she is, she has much experience. _____

(4) I arrived here at six in order that I might teach them English. _____

_____

(5) I hurried lest I should be late for school. _____

(6) This book is so difficult that I cannot read it. _____

(7) This is such a good book that we must read it. _____

(8) This school is bigger than that one. _____

(9) This school is as big as that one. _____

(10) He talks as if he were a teacher. _____

(11) They traveled as far as China. _____

(12) Hardly had she seen me before she ran away. _____

(13) As soon as she saw me, she ran away. _____

(14) However hard you may work, you cannot succeed. _____

_____

(15) Whatever you want to have, I will give you everything. _____

_____

2. 다음 문장을 영작하시오.

(1) 만일 당신이 나를 사랑한다면 나는 당신을 사랑하겠다. _____

_____

(2) 그녀는 너무 부지런해서 모든 사람에게 사랑을 받는다. _____

_____

연습문제

(3) 그녀는 나의 어머니만큼 아름답지 않다. _____

(4) 나는 학교에 늦지 않으려고 일찍 일어났다. _____

(5) 나는 일어나자마자 이를 닦고 세수를 했다. _____

3. 다음 (   ) 안에서 알맞은 말을 고르시오.

(1) He was busy, (and, but) he didn't go to the meeting.

(2) He was busy, (and, but) he went to the meeting.

(3) Study hard, (and, or) you will succeed.

(4) Study hard, (and, or) you will fail.

(5) (Because, For) it is rainy all day, I have to stay at home.

(6) Neither you (or, nor) she is wrong.

(7) I know the first person (who, that) I met in Seoul.

(8) He will be very happy (if, whether) he meets her again.

(9) I didn't know the fact (that, which) he was a teacher.

(10) (Though, As) I am tired, I want to go to bed early.

(11) No sooner had he seen me (than, when) he ran away.

(12) (Unless, If) I have no money, I cannot go abroad.

(13) I don't know (that, whether) she will come soon or not.

(14) I went to the beach (during, while) my summer vacation.

(15) I went on a tour (during, while) I stayed in New York.

4. 다음 (   ) 안에 알맞은 말을 써 넣으시오.

(1) Either she (   ) I am happy.

(2) I cannot understand (   ) you said.

(3) Young (   ) he is, he can do anything.

(4) Now (   ) he is rich, he can buy a nice car.

(5) I worked hard so that I (   ) succeed in my life.

(6) You must hurry lest you (   ) be late for school.

(7) She talks as (   ) she were a doctor.

(8) However hard you (   ) try, you cannot finish your work.

(9) She is not (   ) beautiful as my sister.

(10) He is (   ) a good man that he is loved by everyone.

1. 다음 두 문장의 뜻이 같아지도록 (   ) 안에 알맞은 말을 써 넣으시오.

   (1) As I caught cold, I was absent from school.

       = I caught cold, (   ) I was absent from school.

   (2) Not only he but also I can speak English well.

       = I (   ) (   ) (   ) he can speak English well.

   (3) I don't like either coffee or tea.

       = I like (   ) coffee (   ) tea.

   (4) I don't know whether she will come here soon.

       = I don't know (   ) she will come here soon.

   (5) If you are not busy, you may go to the party.

       = (   ) you are busy, you may go to the party.

   (6) I worked hard so that I might not fail in the work.

       = I worked hard (   ) I (   ) fail in the work.

   (7) No sooner had I entered the room than they stood up.

       = (   ) (   ) (   ) I entered the room, they stood up.

   (8) If it rains tomorrow, I will not go out.

       = (   ) case it rains, I will not go out.

   (9) If you want to meet me, come and see me.

       = If you want to meet me, come (   ) see me.

   (10) No matter how rich you may be, you should not waste money.

       = (   ) rich you may be, you should not waste money.

2. 다음 문장의 밑줄 친 부분의 뜻을 구별하여 우리말로 옮기시오.

   (1) He worked hard <u>so that</u> he <u>might</u> succeed. _____

   (2) He worked <u>so</u> hard <u>that</u> he could succeed. _____

   (3) He worked hard, <u>so that</u> he succeeded. _____

   (4) <u>Either</u> she <u>or</u> I am wrong. _____

   (5) <u>Neither</u> she <u>nor</u> I am wrong. _____

   (6) Work hard, <u>or</u> you will fail. _____

   (7) Work hard, <u>and</u> you will succeed. _____

   (8) I don't know <u>whether</u> she will come soon <u>or not</u>. _____

Part 10

문장 전환

TRANSFORMATION
OF SENTENCES

1. Work hard, **and** you will succeed. [중문 ··· 복문]　　열심히 일하라, 그러면 당신은 성공할 것이다.
   If you work hard, you will succeed.
2. He worked hard, **but he failed**. [중문 ··· 단문]　　그는 열심히 일했다, 그러나 실패하고 말았다.
   He worked hard **only to fail**.
3. She believes **that I am** honest. [복문 ··· 단문]　　그녀는 내가 정직하다고 믿는다.
   She believes **me to be** honest.

문장의 내용을 바꾸지 않고 그 형식만을 문법적으로 바꿔 쓰는 것을 문장의 전환이라고 한다.

1 문장 전환의 여러 가지 형태

1 중문 → 복문 / 복문 → 중문

2 중문 → 단문 / 단문 → 중문

3 단문 → 복문

4 복문 → 단문

5 단문 → 단문 (단어와 품사의 변형)

6 가정법 → 직설법 / 직설법 → 가정법

7 능동태 → 수동태 / 수동태 → 능동태

8 직접화법 → 간접화법 / 간접화법 → 직접화법

9 두 문장을 한 문장으로 결합 (의문대명사, 관계대명사, 관계부사 등을 활용)

10 비교의 문장 전환

11 시제의 문장 전환

12 관용어구의 문장 전환

▶▶ 가정법의 문장 전환, 태의 문장 전환, 화법의 문장 전환, 시제의 문장 전환 등은 앞장 참조

Chapter 01 문장 전환

1 중문 → 복문

P·r·e·v·i·e·w

1. I was tired, **so** I went to bed early.
   As I was tired, I went to bed early.
2. She is poor, **but** she wants to help others.
   Though she is poor, she wants to help others.
3. Come here quickly, **and** I will give it to you.
   If you come here quickly, I will give it to you.

나는 피곤했다. 그래서 나는 잠자리에 일찍 들었다.

그녀는 가난하다. 그러나 그녀는 다른 사람들 돕기를 원한다.

여기로 빨리 오라, 그러면 나는 너에게 그것을 주겠다.

---

1 중문의 so는 복문에서 as(because) 접속사로 바꾼다.
- I didn't have any money, **so** I didn't go to college.
  - ⟹ **As** I didn't have any money, I didn't go to college.
  - ⟹ I didn't go to college **because** I didn't have any money.

2 중문의 and는 복문에서 if 접속사로 바꾼다. 〈명령문, and + 문장〉의 경우
- Study hard, **and** you will succeed.
  - ⟹ **If** you study hard, you will succeed.

3 중문의 or는 복문에서 if ~ not으로 바꾼다. 〈명령문 + or + 문장〉의 경우
- Study hard, **or** you will fail.
  - ⟹ **If** you don't study hard, you will fail.
  - ⟹ **Unless** you study hard, you will fail.

4 중문의 but은 복문에서 though 접속사로 바꾼다.
- He lives near my house, **but** I don't know him well.
  - ⟹ **Though** he lives near my house, I don't know him well.

5 중문의 and then은 복문에서 after 접속사로 바꾼다.
- She did her homework, **and then** she watched TV.
  - ⟹ **After** she did her homework, she watched TV.

6 중문의 for는 복문에서 as 접속사로 바꾼다.
- He was absent from school, **for** he was sick.
  - ⟹ **As** he was sick, he was absent from school.

Part 10 문장 전환 Transformation of Sentences

2 중문 → 단문

1. She is very old, **and** she cannot walk for a long time.
   She is **too** old **to** walk for a long time.
2. He tried his best, **but** he failed in the examination.
   He tried his best **only to** fail in the examination.
3. You must work hard, **or** you will not succeed.
   Without working hard, you will not succeed.
4. I can speak **not only** English **but also** French.
   I can speak French **as well as** English.

그녀는 매우 나이가 많다, 그래서 그녀는 오랫동안 걸을 수 없다.

그는 최선을 다했다, 그러나 시험에 실패했다.

당신은 열심히 일해야만 한다, 그렇지 않으면 성공할 수 없을 것이다.
나는 영어뿐만 아니라 불어도 말할 수 있다.

---

1 중문의 and는 단문에서

① too ~ to, enough to로 바꿀 수 있다.
② 분사를 써서 바꿀 수 있다.
③ 동명사를 써서 바꿀 수 있다.
④ 부정사의 결과를 써서 바꿀 수 있다.
⑤ 특별한 표현법을 써서 바꿀 수 있다.

· He is very poor, **and** he cannot stand it any more.
  ➡ He is **too** poor **to** stand it any more.

· He is very rich, **and** he can buy an airplane.
  ➡ He is rich **enough to** buy an airplane.

· The train leaves Busan at six, **and** arrives in Seoul at ten.
  ➡ The train leaves Busan at six, **arriving** in Seoul at ten.

· Her son was a police officer, **and** she is proud of it.
  ➡ She is proud of her son **having been** a police officer.

· She grew up **and** became a scientist.
  ➡ She grew up **to become** a scientist.

· Knowing is one thing, **and** teaching is quite another.
  ➡ Knowing is **quite different from** teaching.

· The book was written easily, **and** it was sold well.
  ➡ **Written** easily, the book was sold well.

162

2 중문의 but은 단문에서

① 부정사의 결과(only to)를 써서 바꿀 수 있다.
② 전치사구 뒤에 동명사를 써서 바꿀 수 있다.
③ 특별한 표현법을 써서 바꿀 수 있다.

· I worked hard, **but** I failed to finish the work.
   ➡ I worked hard **only to** fail to finish the work.

· She was excited, **but** she kept her temper.
   ➡ **In spite of being** excited, she kept her temper.
   ➡ **In spite of** her excitement, she kept her temper.

· He did **not** try to study **but** wanted to play outside.
   ➡ **Instead of trying** to study, he wanted to play outside.

· I walked for a long time, **but** I was not tired.
   ➡ I walked for a long time **without being** tired.

· I **not only** teach English, **but** write English books.
   ➡ **Besides** teaching English, I write English books.
   ➡ **In addition to** teaching English, I write English books.

· He **hoped to succeed**, **but** he **failed**.
   ➡ He **hoped to have succeeded**.

· She searched for her friend's house, **but** could not find it.
   ➡ She searched for her friend's house **in vain**.

3 중문의 or는 단문에서

① 부정사를 써서 바꿀 수 있다.
② 전치사를 써서 바꿀 수 있다.

· Get up early, **or** you will be late for school.
   ➡ Get up early **not to** be late for school.

· You must not eat too much, or you will be punished.
   ➡ You must not eat too much **to escape** being punished.

· Work hard, **or** you will fail.
   ➡ **Without** working hard, you will fail.

4 중문의 so는 단문에서

① 분사구를 써서 바꿀 수 있다.
② 전치사(구)를 써서 바꿀 수 있다.
③ 부정사를 써서 바꿀 수 있다.

- I have no friend, **so** I am not happy.
  ➡ **Having** no friend, I am not happy.

- She is poor, so she cannot help him.
  ➡ **On account of being** poor, she cannot help him.

- He wanted to marry her, **so** he persuaded her.
  ➡ He persuaded her **in order to** marry her.

5 중문의 for는 단문에서

① 동명사를 써서 바꿀 수 있다.
② 전치사(구)를 써서 바꿀 수 있다.
③ 특별한 표현법을 써서 바꿀 수 있다.

- She was scolded, **for** she stayed out too late.
  ➡ She was scolded **for** staying out too late.

- He was praised, **for** he helped an old woman on the street.
  ➡ He was praised **for** helping an old woman on the street.

- He was absent from school, **for** he was sick.
  ➡ He was absent from school **because of** his sickness.

- His father was disappointed, for he failed in the examination.
  ➡ **To his father's disappointment**, he failed in the examination.

Pattern Practice

1. Work hard, **and** you will succeed in life.

2. Work hard, **or** you will fail in life.

3. He is poor, **but** he wants his son to go to college.

4. He is very busy, **so** he can not go to the meeting.

5. The lions caught the deer, **for** they were very hungry.

6. She finished her homework, **and then** watched a movie on TV.

7. **If** you work hard, you will succeed in life.

8. **Unless** you work hard, you will fail in life.

9. **Though** he is poor, he wants his son to go to college.

10. **As** she was very busy, she couldn't go to the meeting.

11. **As** the lions were very hungry, they caught the deer.

12. **After** he had finished his homework, he watched a movie on TV.

13. **If** you don't win the game, you will be punished by your coach.

14. Young **as** he is, he has much experience.

15. **Wherever** you may go, I will follow you.

16. She is very idle, **and** she cannot get the job.

17. She is very diligent, **and** she will succeed.

18. The express bus starts at seven **and** arrives at Chungju at nine.

19. He grew up **and** became a pilot.

20. The English book was not difficult, **and** it was sold very well.

21. He studied very hard, **but** he failed to pass the examination.

22. He was tired, **but** he finished the work.

23. He did **not** watch TV, **but** studied English hard.

24. He **not only** teaches English, **but also** writes English books.

25. He **expected to marry** her, **but** he failed to marry her.

26. Hurry up, **or** you will miss the bus.

27. Work hard, **or** you will fail.

28. She has no friend to play with, **so** she is unhappy.

29. She wanted to go to college, **so** she studied very hard.

30. She is ill, **so** she cannot study any more.

31. He was absent from school, **for** he was sick.

32. He is **too** old **to** go out alone at night.

33. He studied hard **only to fail** in the examination.

34. **Without** working hard, you will fail.

35. **On account of** being poor, he cannot go to college.

1. 다음 영문을 우리말로 옮기시오.

(1) Get up early, and you will catch the first bus.

_____

(2) Get up early, or you will be late for school.

_____

(3) He is tired, but he has to finish the work.

_____

(4) Though I was busy, I wrote to my mother once a month.

_____

(5) As my friend was sick, he could not go to the mountain with me.

_____

(6) She has been ill for a week, so she cannot continue the work.

_____

(7) If you don't read many books, you will not have much knowledge.

_____

(8) Unless you study hard, you cannot enter the college.

_____

(9) Wherever you may go, you will be welcomed.

_____

(10) I hoped to have succeeded.

_____

(11) She worked very hard only to fail in the business.

_____

(12) The express train starts from Seoul at six, arriving in Busan at eleven.

_____

(13) I don't like such a man, for he is idle and dishonest.

_____

(14) Old as she is, she can do such a work.

_____

(15) He not only writes a poem, but sells a car.

_____

2. 다음 문장을 영작하시오.

(1) 부지런하라, 그러면 성공할 것이다.

_____

(2) 그 일을 마치도록 노력하라, 그렇지 않으면 너는 불행할 것이다.

_____

(3) 나는 어제 피곤해서 잠자리에 일찍 들었다.

_____

(4) 바쁘지만 너를 만나러 가겠다.

_____

(5) 내일 비가 온다면 나는 집에 머물러 있겠다.

_____

3. 다음 중문을 복문으로 바꾸시오.

(1) She lives near my house, but she doesn't know me.

_____

(2) He studied hard, so he passed the examination.

_____

(3) Get up early, and you will not be late for school.

_____

(4) Don't be late for school, or you will be punished by your teacher.

_____

(5) He finished the work, and then he went to the movies.

_____

(6) She cannot go to the party, for she is very busy.

_____

4. 다음 중문을 단문으로 바꾸시오.

(1) His father is very rich, and he can go abroad to study more.

_____

(2) The train leaves Incheon at six and arrives in Seoul at ten.

_____

(3) He grew up and became a pilot.

_____

(4) She worked hard, but she failed in the business.

_____

(5) She was excited, but she kept his temper.

_____

(6) He not only teaches English, but writes English books.

_____

(7) I hoped to meet her, but I didn't.

_____

(8) He was absent from school, for he was ill.

_____

(9) I have no house to live in, so I am unhappy.

_____

(10) His brother is very young, and he cannot go to school.

_____

(11) Work hard, or you will fail in life.

_____

(12) The English book was written easily, and it was sold well.

_____

(13) Knowing is one thing and teaching is quite another.

_____

(14) I am poor, so I cannot help them.

_____

3 단문 → 복문

1. She expects **to succeed**.
   She expects **that she will succeed**.

   그녀는 성공하리라 기대한다.

2. He is proud of his father **being a teacher**.
   He is proud **that his father is a teacher**.

   그는 아버지가 선생님인 것을 자랑스럽게 여긴다.

3. **Having no money**, he can not buy the house.
   As he has no money, he can not buy the house.

   돈이 없어서, 그는 집을 살 수 없다.

4. Would you tell me **the time** of your arrival?
   Would you tell me **the time when you will arrive**?

   당신의 도착 시간을 말씀해주시겠습니까?

5. **Because of the rain**, I stayed at home.
   I stayed at home **because it rained**.

   비 때문에 나는 집에 있었다.

---

1 부정사를 접속사 that을 써서 명사절로 바꾼다.

① 〈(think, believe, find, know) + 목적어 + to부정사〉
   to부정사를 접속사 that이 이끄는 명사절로 바꾼다.

   · I think her **to be** honest.
      ➡ I think **that** she **is** honest.

   · I believe her **to have been** honest.
      ➡ I believe **that** she **was** honest.

② 〈(expect, wish, intend) + 목적어 + to부정사〉
   to부정사를 that 명사절로 바꾸고 시제는 미래 시제로 한다.

   · I expect **to succeed**.
      ➡ I expect **that I shall** succeed.

   · I expect him **to succeed**.
      ➡ I expect **that** he **will** succeed.

주의

hope는 목적보어를 가질 수 없지만 that절은 가질 수 있다.
   · I hope him to succeed. (×)
   · I hope that he will succeed. (○)
want는 목적보어를 가질 수 있지만 that절은 가질 수 없다.
   · I want him to succeed. (○)
   · I want that he will succeed. (×)

③ 〈(expect, intend, hope, want 등의 과거) + 완료부정사〉
완료부정사는 과거의 뜻을 이루지 못한 의지 희망을 나타낸다.

- I **hoped to have seen** you at the party yesterday.
    ➡ I **hoped to see** you at the party yesterday, but I didn't.

- I **wanted to have married** her last year.
    ➡ I **wanted to marry** her last year, but I didn't.

④ 〈(seem, appear, prove, be said, be believed, be thought) + 부정사〉
to부정사를 접속사 that이 이끄는 명사절(진주어)로 바꾸고 가주어 It을 문두에 놓는다.
[It ~ that ~]의 구문을 취한다.

- She **seems to be** rich.
    ➡ It **seems** that she **is** rich.

- She **seems to have been** rich.
    ➡ It **seems** that she **was** rich.

- He **is said to be** a pilot.
    ➡ It **is said** that he is a pilot.

- He **was said to have been** a pilot.
    ➡ It **was said** that he **had been** a pilot.

⑤ 〈It is ~ for + 사람(목적격) + to부정사〉
to부정사를 접속사 that이 이끄는 명사절로 바꾼다.

- It is impossible **for him to make** such a thing.
    ➡ It is impossible **that** he **should** make such a thing.

- It is strange **for a child to say** so.
    ➡ It is strange **that** a child **should** say so.
    ▶▶ 이성적 판단: impossible, important, necessary, natural, wrong, right, good 등이 오면 종속절에 should를 쓰고 should는 해석하지 않는다.
    ▶▶ 감정적 판단: strange, surprising, regrettable, wonderful 등이 오면 종속절에 should를 쓰고 should는 '~하다니'로 해석한다.

⑥ 5형식에서 〈동사 + it(가목적어) + 형용사(명사) + to부정사(진목적어)〉
to부정사를 접속사 that이 이끄는 명사절로 바꾼다.

- I think it easy **to read** this book.
    ➡ I think **that it** is easy **to read** this book.

- I found **it** impossible **to write** a book in a month.
    ➡ I found **that it** is impossible **to write** a book in a month.

2 동명사가 있는 구를 접속사 that을 써서 명사절로 바꾼다.

① of, at, on 등의 전치사를 빼고 접속사 that이 이끄는 명사절로 바꾼다.

- I am sure **of** his **being** honest.
  - ⇒ I am sure **that** he is honest.

- I was proud **of being** a teacher.
  - ⇒ I was proud **that** I **was** a teacher.

- I insist **on** Tom **being punished**.
  - ⇒ I insist **that** Tom should **be punished**.
  - ▶▶동명사가 수동태일 때 의미상 주어에 's를 붙이지 못한다.

- I didn't know the fact **of there being** a man in the room.
  - ⇒ I didn't know the fact **that there was** a man in the room.
  - ▶▶ the fact가 동격 명사이므로 of 이하와는 동격이다. 유도부사 there를 써야 한다.

② 〈명사(대명사)의 소유격+명사〉를 접속사 that이 이끄는 명사절로 바꾼다. 이때 소유격이 주어가 되고 명사는 형용사나 동사로 바꾼다.

- I am sure **of her honesty**.
  - ⇒ I am sure **that she is honest**.

- I am sure **of her success**.
  - ⇒ I am sure **that she will succeed**.

- I believe **her innocence**.
  - ⇒ I believe **that she is innocent**.

- I doubt **the truth of her statement**.
  - ⇒ I doubt **if her statement is true**.

3 〈명사 + 형용사구(전치사 + 명사)〉를 의문사로 시작되는 명사절로 바꾼다.

문장의 내용이 의문이 있을 때 내용에 따라 when, where, why, what, who 등을 써서 명사절을 만든다.

- Do you know **the day of his departure**?
  - ⇒ Do you know **when he will depart**?

- I don't know **the place of his birth**.
  - ⇒ I don't know **where he was born**.

- Can you tell me **the reason for her refusal**?
  - ⇒ Can you tell me **why she refused**?

4 〈의문사 + to부정사〉를 의문사로 시작되는 명사절로 바꾼다.

의문사절의 주어는 주절의 주어로 하고 should를 쓴다.

- I don't know **what to do** next.
  - ⇒ I don't know **what I should** do next.

Pattern Practice

1. I **think her to be** wise.

2. I **found him to have been** diligent.

3. I **wish to marry** her.

4. I **wish him to marry** her.

5. I **hoped to have seen** him yesterday.

6. She **seems to be** happy.

7. She **seems to have been** happy.

8. He **was believed to be** honest.

9. He **was believed to have been** honest.

10. It is **necessary for her to learn** English.

11. It is **strange for a boy to say** so.

12. I **think it** difficult **for her to read** this book.

13. I am sure **of** his **being** good.

14. I was proud **of being** a doctor.

15. I am sure **of his honesty**.

16. Do you know **when to start?**

17. I don't know **the day of his departure**.

18. She insisted **on** my **being punished**.

19. I don't know **what to do** next.

20. I don't know **the reason for her refusal**.

1. 다음 영문을 우리말로 옮기시오.

(1) I believe him to be honest. _____

(2) I think him to have been dishonest. _____

(3) I expect to succeed. _____

(4) I expected to succeed. _____

(5) I hoped to have passed the examination. _____

(6) She was said to be a doctor. _____

(7) It is impossible for her to write a book. _____

(8) I think it easy to read the book. _____

(9) She is proud of her son being a doctor. _____

(10) I don't know where to go. _____

(11) I want him to learn English. _____

(12) I believe his innocence. _____

(13) I don't know the place of his birth. _____

(14) It is surprising for her to do such a thing. _____

(15) I found it impossible to write a book in a month. _____

2. 다음 문장을 영작하시오.

(1) 나는 그가 성공하기를 원한다. _____

(2) 나는 그가 성공하리라 확신한다. _____

(3) 나는 영어를 배우는 것이 어렵다고 생각한다. _____

(4) 나는 다음에 무엇을 해야 할지 모르겠다. _____

(5) 그녀가 일주일에 책 한 권을 다 읽는 것은 불가능하다. _____

3. 다음 단문을 복문으로 바꾸시오.

(1) I expect to succeed.

_____

(2) I expect him to succeed.

_____

(3) I expected to succeed.

_____

(4) I expected him to succeed.

_____

(5) I think her to be honest.

_____

(6) She is said to be honest.

_____

(7) She was said to be honest.

_____

(8) He is believed to have been diligent.

_____

(9) He was believed to have been diligent.

_____

(10) I am sure of her being wise.

_____

(11) I found it right to do so.

_____

(12) It is impossible for her to speak Korean.

_____

(13) I don't know what to do next.

_____

(14) I doubt the truth of his statement.

_____

(15) I am sure of his success.

_____

(16) I don't know the place of her birth.

_____

(17) I insisted on his studying English hard.

_____

(18) It is strange for her to say so.

_____

(19) She is proud of her son being a doctor.

_____

(20) She is proud of her son having been a doctor.

_____

5 부정사를 관계대명사를 써서 형용사절로 바꾼다.

① 〈명사 + to부정사〉를 관계대명사로 시작되는 형용사절로 바꾼다.

- He was **the first Korean to fly** across the Pacific.
  ➡ He was **the first Korean that flew across the Pacific**.

- Tom had no **friend to play** with.
  ➡ Tom had no **friend with whom he would play**.

- Mrs. Brown has no **friend to help** her.
  ➡ Mrs. Brown has no **friend who will help her**.

- This is **the book to read**.
  ➡ This is **the book which we should read**.

② 〈명사 + for + 목적격 + to부정사〉를 관계대명사로 시작되는 형용사절로 바꾼다.

- There are **a lot of things for you to do**.
  ➡ There are **a lot of things that you should do**.

- This is not **the book for him to read**.
  ➡ This is not **the book which he will read**.

6 부정사를 관계부사로 시작되는 형용사절로 바꾼다.

① 〈명사 + to부정사〉를 관계부사로 시작되는 형용사절로 바꾼다.

- This is **the time to start** right now.
  ➡ This is **the time when we should start right now**.

- Do you know **the place to go**?
  ➡ Do you know **the place where you should go**?

② 〈명사 + for + 목적격 + to부정사〉를 관계부사로 시작하는 형용사절로 바꾼다.

- I don't know **the reason for her to resign**.
  ➡ I don't know **the reason why she should resign**.

- Do you know **how to drive** a car?
  ➡ Do you know **the way that you should drive a car**?

7 〈형용사 + 명사〉, 〈명사 + 형용사구〉를 관계사로 시작되는 형용사절로 바꾼다.

① 〈형용사 + 명사〉를 관계사로 시작되는 형용사절로 바꾼다.

- The **diligent man** will succeed.
  ➡ **The man who is diligent** will succeed.

· **My answer** is right.

　⇒ **The answer that I made** is right.

② 〈명사 + 형용사구(전치사 + 명사)〉를 관계사로 시작되는 형용사절로 바꾼다.

　· I know **a person of wisdom**.

　　⇒ I know a person who is wise. (= I know a wise person.)

8 부정사를 접속사 that을 써서 부사절로 바꾼다.

① so as to, in order to 등의 부정사를 so that ~ may로 바꾼다.

　· I work **so as to succeed** in my life.

　　⇒ I work **so that** I **may succeed** in my life.

　· She studied **in order to pass** the examination.

　　⇒ She studied **so that** she **might pass** the examination.

　· My sister hurried **not to be** late for school.

　　⇒ My sister hurried **so that** he **might not be** late for school.

② so ~ as to의 부정사를 so ~ that으로 바꾼다.

　· He worked **so** hard **as to succeed** in life.

　　⇒ He worked **so** hard **that** he **succeeded** in life.

　· She is **so kind as to lend** me her book.

　　⇒ She is **so** kind **that** she **lends** me her book.

③ too ~ to의 부정사를 so ~ that ~ cannot으로 바꾼다.

　· He is **too** old **to go** to the mountain alone.

　　⇒ He is **so** old **that** he **cannot go** to the mountain alone.

　· The book is **too** difficult for her **to read**.

　　⇒ The book is **so** difficult **that** she **cannot read** it.

④ enough to의 부정사를 so ~ that ~ can으로 바꾼다.

　· She is kind **enough to show** me the way to the station.

　　⇒ She is **so** kind **that** she **can show** me the way to the station.

　· Her father was rich **enough** for her **to go** to college.

　　⇒ Her father was **so** rich that she **could go** to college.

　· He is **too** clever **not to understand** the fact.

　　⇒ He is **so** clever **that** he **can understand** the fact.

9 부정사를 접속사 if를 써서 부사절로 바꾼다.

부정사가 조건을 나타낼 때는 if절로 바꾼다.

- I should be happy **to see** her again.
  ➡ I should be happy **if I see her again**.

10 분사구문을 부사절로 바꾼다.

① 때를 나타내는 접속사 when, while 등을 써서 부사절로 바꾼다.

- **Walking** along the street, I met Mr. Brown.
  ➡ **While I was walking** along the street, I met Mr. Brown.

- **Seeing** a police officer, he ran away.
  ➡ **When he saw** a police officer, he ran away.

② 원인, 이유를 나타내는 접속사 as, because, since 등을 써서 부사절로 바꾼다.

- **Being** busy, I could not go to the party.
  ➡ **As I was** busy, I could not go to the party.

- **Having been** sick, I was absent from school yesterday.
  ➡ **Because I had been** sick, I was absent from school yesterday.

③ 조건을 나타내는 접속사 if를 써서 부사절로 바꾼다.

- **Turning** to the right, you will find the building.
  ➡ **If** you **turn** to the right, you will find the building.

④ 양보를 나타내는 접속사 though, although 등을 써서 부사절로 바꾼다.

- **Living** in an apartment, I don't meet him.
  ➡ **Though I live** in an apartment, I don't meet him.

⑤ 계속을 나타내는 접속사 and를 써서 부사절로 바꾼다.

- The train leaves Seoul at six, **arriving** in Busan at ten.
  ➡ The train leaves Seoul at six, **and** it **arrives** in Busan at ten.

11 동명사를 when, as soon as 등을 써서 부사절로 바꾼다.

① ⟨in + ~ing⟩의 부사구를 when으로 시작되는 부사절로 바꾼다.

- **In choosing** friends, we cannot be too careful.
  ➡ **When we choose** friends, we cannot be too careful.

② 〈on + ~ing〉의 부사구를 as soon as로 시작되는 부사절로 바꾼다.

· **On seeing** me, she ran away.
  ➡ **As soon as she saw** me, she ran away.

③ 〈never ~ without + ~ing〉를 whenever, when을 써서 부사절로 바꾼다.

· My uncle **never** come home **without buying** me some cake.
  ➡ **Whenever** my uncle comes home, he buys me some cake.
  ➡ **When** my uncle comes home, he always buys me some cake.

12 명사, 대명사를 when, while, as soon as로 시작되는 부사절로 바꾼다.

① 〈on + 명사〉를 when, as soon as로 시작되는 부사절로 바꾼다.

· **On my return** in the afternoon, my friend was waiting for me.
  ➡ **When I returned** in the afternoon, my friend was waiting for me.

· **On his arrival**, she went out.
  ➡ **As soon as** he arrived, she went out.

② 〈during + 명사〉를 while로 시작되는 부사절로 바꾼다.

· **During my stay** in Seoul, I wanted to learn Korean.
  ➡ While **I was staying** in Seoul, I wanted to learn Korean.

13 전치사구를 부사절로 바꾼다.

① because of(on account of = owing to)를 as로 시작되는 부사절로 바꾼다.

· **On account of** illness, I was absent from school.
  ➡ **As I was ill**, I was absent from school.

② in spite of(despite = for all = not withstanding)를 though로 시작되는 부사절로 바꾼다.

· **In spite of** the rain, I went on a picnic.
  ➡ **Though it rained**, I went on a picnic.

③ but for를 if로 시작되는 부사절로 바꾼다.

· **But for** your help, I would not succeed.
  ➡ **If it were not for** your help, I would not succeed.

Pattern Practice

1. He is the first man **to swim** across the Han River.

2. This is the book **for him to read**.

3. I have no friend **to play with**.

4. She has no one **to help** her.

5. This is the time **to start** right now.

6. I don't know the place **to go**.

7. I don't know the reason **for him to resign**.

8. Can you tell me **how to drive** a car?

9. The **diligent** man will succeed.

10. I know a person **of wisdom**.

11. She got up early **so as to catch** the first train.

12. She studies hard **in order to pass** the examination.

13. I hurried **not to be** late for school.

14. He got up **so** early **as to catch** the first train.

15. He is **too** weak **to walk** for a long time.

16. This book is **too** difficult **for him to read**.

17. She is kind **enough to tell** me the news.

18. I should be happy **to see** her again.

19. **Walking** along the street, I met him.

20. **Being** tired, I want to go to bed early tonight.

21. **Turning** to the right, you will find the hospital.

22. **Living** next door, I don't know Mr. Brown.

23. **It being** fine today, I want to go on a picnic.

24. My car leaves Seoul at seven, **arriving** in Incheon at eight.

25. **In choosing** a good book, you must be careful.

26. **On seeing** me, he ran away.

27. He **never** comes home **without buying** me some cake.

28. **On my return**, she went out.

29. **During my stay** in America, I wanted to learn English.

30. **On his arrival**, she went out.

1. 다음 영문을 우리말로 옮기시오.

(1) He is the first Korean to fly across the Pacific. _____

(2) This is the book for me to read. _____

(3) He is a man of importance. _____

(4) I got up early so as not to be late for the meeting. _____

(5) This book is too difficult for her to read. _____

(6) This book is easy enough for her to read. _____

(7) He got up early so as to catch the first bus. _____

(8) He got up so early as to catch the first bus. _____

(9) Meeting her friend, she was very happy. _____

(10) Being diligent, she can succeed. _____

(11) Turning to your right, you will find the building. _____

(12) Being young, she has much experience. _____

(13) On seeing a police officer, he ran away. _____

(14) My father never comes home without buying me some candy. _____

_____

(15) Being interesting, the book is sold very well. _____

2. 다음 문장을 영작하시오.

(1) 거리를 따라 걷고 있는 동안 나는 그녀를 만났다. _____

(2) 비가 와서 나는 외출을 포기했다. _____

(3) 그 소식을 듣자마자 그는 깜짝 놀랐다. _____

(4) 당신의 도움이 없다면 그는 성공할 수 없을 텐데. _____

(5) 나는 어디로 가야 할지 모른다. _____

3. 다음 단문을 복문으로 바꾸시오.

(1) This is the man to write an English book.

_____

(2) I know the lady reading a newspaper in the room.

_____

(3) This is the book for her to read.

_____

(4) Can you tell me the reason for him to refuse the proposal?

_____

(5) His father worked hard so as to finish the work.

_____

(6) He hurries in order not to be late for school.

_____

(7) She is too clever not to understand the fact.

_____

(8) She is kind enough to show me the way to the post office.

_____

(9) I should be happy to go abroad to study more.

_____

(10) Playing tennis, I made a friend.

_____

(11) Having no money, I cannot lend him any.

_____

(12) Going to the park right now, you will meet her.

_____

(13) Living in the apartment, I don't know Mr. Kim.

_____

(14) It being fine today, I will paly tennis.

_____

(15) In choosing a friend, you must be very careful.

_____

(16) On seeing me, he stood up and went out.

_____

(17) My father never comes home without buying me some cake.

_____

(18) My car leaves Seoul at six, arriving in Busan at eleven. (중문으로)

_____

(19) I respect a person of wisdom.

_____

(20) The honest man will be loved by everyone.

_____

4 복문 → 단문

1 종속절을 부정사를 써서 단문으로 바꾼다.

① 종속절이 명사절일 때

· She expects **that she will** succeed.
➡ She expects **to succeed.**

· It seems **that he is honest.**
➡ He seems **to be** honest.

· It is possible **that he should pass the examination.**
➡ It is possible **for him to pass** the examination.

② 종속절이 형용사절일 때

· He was the first Korean **that flew across the Pacific.**
➡ He was the first Korean **to fly** across the Pacific.

· There are a lot of books **that I should read.**
➡ There are a lot of books **for me to read.**

③ 종속절이 부사절일 때

· He worked hard **so that he might succeed.**
➡ He worked hard **so as to succeed.**

· He worked so hard **that he succeeded.**
➡ He worked so hard **as to succeed.**

· This book is so difficult **that I cannot read it.**
➡ This book is **too** difficult **for me to read.**

· She is so old **that she cannot climb the mountain.**
➡ She is **too** old **to climb the mountain.**

· His father was so rich **that he could go to college.**
➡ His father was rich **enough for him to go to college.**

· I was very happy **as I saw him.**
➡ I was very happy **to see him.**

· I should be glad **if I meet her.**
➡ I should be glad **to meet her.**

· She steps aside **so that the fat lady may pass by.**
➡ She steps aside **for the fat lady to pass by.**

2 종속절을 동명사를 써서 단문으로 바꾼다.

① 종속절이 명사절일 때

· He is proud **that his son is a teacher**.
➡ He is proud **of his son('s) being** a teacher.

· I know **that she studies Chinese**.
➡ I know **of her studying** Chinese.

· I forget **that I wrote him a letter**.
➡ I forget **writing** him a letter.

② 종속절이 형용사절일 때

· There is no reason **why he should refuse the proposal**.
➡ There is no reason **for his refusing** the proposal.

· She showed me a picture **which she had painted herself**.
➡ She showed me a picture **of her own painting**.

③ 종속절이 부사절일 때

· You must be careful **when you cross the street**.
➡ You must be careful **in crossing** the street.

· **As soon as he saw me**, he ran away.
➡ **On seeing** me, he ran away.

· **After you have finished the work**, you may go out.
➡ **After having finished** the work, you may go out.

3 종속절은 분사를 써서 단문으로 바꾼다.

① 종속절이 형용사절일 때

· People **who live in the country** live long.
➡ People **living** in the country live long.

· Do you know a boy **who is playing baseball**
➡ Do you know a boy **playing** baseball?

· I bought a watch **which was made in Korea**.
➡ I bought a watch **made** in Korea.

② 종속절이 부사절일 때

· **As I was busy**, I could not go to the meeting.
  ➡ **Being** busy, I could not go to the meeting.

· **As it is fine today**, I want to go on a picnic.
  ➡ It being fine today, I want to go on a picnic.

· **After she had finished the work**, she went out.
  ➡ **Having finished** the work, she went out.

4 종속절을 전치사구를 써서 단문으로 바꾼다.

① 때의 접속사 when, while 등은 in, during 등으로 바꾼다.

· **When you write a book**, you must be careful.
  You must be careful **in writing a book**.

· **While I was studying**, my brother didn't make a noise.
  During my studying, my brother didn't make a noise.

② 원인의 접속사 because를 because of, on account of 등으로 바꾼다.

· I was at home **because it was rainy**.
  I was at home **because of the rain**.

③ 양보의 접속사 though를 in spite of로 바꾼다.

· She has failed **though I helped her**.
  She has failed **in spite of my helping her**.

④ 조건의 접속사 if, unless 등을 but for로 바꾼다.

· **If it were not for water**, we could not live any more.
  ➡ **But for water**, we could not live any more.

5 품사 전환에 의한 문장 전환

1 명사로 전환한다.

· She can **play** the piano **very well**.
  ➡ She is **a very good pianist**.

· He **speaks** English **well**.
  ➡ He is **a good speaker of** English.

2 동사, 조동사로 전환한다.

- It is **possible that** we should climb the highest mountain.
  - ➡ We **can climb** the highest mountain.

- He went to church **in haste**.
  - ➡ He **hastened** to go to church.

3 형용사로 전환한다.

- It **rained** all day long.
  - ➡ It was **rainy** all day long.

- Our customs **differ** from yours.
  - ➡ Our customs **are different** from yours.

4 부사로 전환한다.

- We can learn English **with ease**.
  - ➡ We can learn English **easily**.

- I met him at the party **by accident**.
  - ➡ I met him at the party **accidentally**.

Pattern Practice

1. He expects that he will succeed.

2. It seems that he is busy.

3. I have a lot of books that I should read.

4. I work hard so that I may succeed.

5. It is impossible that he should read the book in a week.

6. She is so old that she cannot walk for a long time.

7. She is so wise that she can understand the matter.

8. The book is so difficult that I cannot read it.

9. He steps aside so that she may pass by.

10. He is proud that his father is a teacher.

11. I remember that I wrote her a letter yesterday.

12. I remember that I must write her a letter.

13. You must be careful when you choose a friend.

14. As soon as he saw me, he ran into the room.

15. I know the lady who is playing the piano.

16. I bought a car which was made in Korea.

17. As I was tired, I could not go to his birthday party.

18. After he had finished the work, he watched TV.

19. She failed though she worked hard.

20. If it had not been for his help, she would have failed.

1. 다음 영문을 우리말로 옮기시오.

(1) It is said that she was a teacher and poet.

_____

(2) It is natural that she should not marry such a man.

_____

(3) She worked hard so that she could buy a house.

_____

(4) He is so old that he cannot support his family.

_____

(5) The mountain is so high that we cannot climb it.

_____

(6) He is so wise that everyone wants to listen to his opinions.

_____

(7) He worked so hard that he made much money.

_____

(8) The gold watch which is on the table is hers.

_____

(9) The boy who is playing tennis is my brother.

_____

(10) He insisted that I should win the prize in the speech contest.

_____

(11) There is no reason why she should get angry.

_____

(12) If it were not for water, we could not live any longer.

_____

(13) As I was busy, I could not go to the meeting.

_____

(14) As soon as I finished my homework, I went to bed.

_____

(15) I didn't go out because it was very cold.

_____

연습문제

2. 다음 문장을 영작하시오.

(1) 그는 정직한 것으로 믿어진다.

_____

(2) 비 때문에 나는 하루 종일 집에 있었다.

_____

(3) 나는 너무 피곤해서 잠자리에 들기를 원한다.

_____

(4) 나는 대학을 가기 위해서 열심히 공부했다.

_____

(5) 그녀는 딸이 피아니스트인 것을 자랑스러워한다.

_____

3. 다음 복문을 단문으로 바꾸시오.

(1) She expects that she will get a job.

_____

(2) She expects that I shall get a job.

_____

(3) She expected that she would get a job.

_____

(4) It seems that he was a writer.

_____

(5) This is the man who teaches us English.

_____

(6) I know a boy who is playing baseball.

_____

(7) The book which was written by Shakespeare is famous.

_____

(8) I don't know what I should do next.

_____

(9) He did his best so that he might make her happy.

_____

(10) She was so tired that she could not walk for a long time.

_____

(11) The rock is so heavy that he cannot lift it.

_____

(12) She is so kind that she can show me the way to the hospital.

_____

(13) He is proud that he is a musician.

_____

(14) She is proud that her mother was a famous pianist.

_____

(15) The house which is on the hill is beautiful.

_____

(16) I remember that I must send him some flowers.

_____

(17) As he has a lot of money, he can buy his son an airplane.

_____

(18) As it was rainy yesterday, I could not go to the party.

_____

(19) As soon as he saw me, he ran away.

_____

(20) It is impossible that she should read the book through a week.

_____

1. 다음 두 문장의 뜻이 같아지도록 밑줄 친 부분에 알맞은 말을 써 넣으시오.

   (1) I believed him to be diligent.

   I believed _____ .

   (2) I am sure of his coming.

   I am sure _____ .

   (3) This was the first person to come to the meeting.

   This was the first person _____ .

   (4) I know the girl playing baseball on the playground.

   I know the girl _____ .

   (5) The book is too difficult for her to read.

   The book is _____ .

   (6) Walking along the street, I met Mrs. Kim.

   _____ , I met Mrs. Kim.

   (7) On seeing a police officer, he ran away.

   _____ , he ran away.

   (8) She studied hard only to fail in the examination.

   She studied hard _____ .

   (9) He was ill, so he could not go to her birthday party.

   _____ , he could not go to her birthday party.

   (10) It was raining heavily, but he started for Busan.

   _____ he started for Busan.

   (11) She seems to be happy.

   _____ she is happy.

   (12) He expects me to succeed.

   He expects _____ .

   (13) I go to church by bus on Sunday.

   I go to church _____ a bus on Sunday.

   (14) I know a man of wisdom.

   I know a _____ .

   (15) Shall he carry this bag?

   Shall _____ carry this bag?

   (16) The rain prevented me from going to the party.

   _____ I didn't go to the party.

해답

1. 다음 동사의 과거, 과거분사형을 (　) 안에 써 넣으시오.

(1) played – played　　(2) lived – lived

(3) studied – studied　(4) stopped – stopped

(5) visited – visited　(6) became – become

(7) welcomed – welcomed

(8) said – said　　　　(9) wrote – written

(10) read – read

(11) lay – lain or lied – lied

(12) laid – laid　　　(13) found – found

(14) founded – founded (15) was – been

(16) were – been　　　(17) was – been

(18) had – had　　　　(19) had – had

(20) made – made

2. 다음 동사의 현재분사형을 (　) 안에 써 넣으시오.

(1) playing　　　　　(2) studying

(3) coming　　　　　(4) lying

(5) running　　　　　(6) beginning

(7) visiting　　　　　(8) writing

(9) swimming　　　　(10) dying

1. 다음 영문을 우리말로 옮기시오.

(1) 그는 나의 이름과 주소를 안다.

(2) 그는 영어를 매우 열심히 공부한다.

(3) 그녀는 매일 아침 6시 30분에 학교에 간다.

(4) 태양은 지구보다 더 크다.

(5) 그녀는 내일 집에 도착한다.

(6) 나는 내일 날씨가 좋으면 소풍을 가겠다.

(7) 나는 그가 여기를 떠날 때 여기에 머물겠다.

(8) 나는 그가 여기를 떠날지 모르겠다.

(9) 나는 그가 언제 여기를 떠날지 모르겠다.

(10) 그녀는 수업 중에 종종 졸곤 했다.

(11) 그는 아침 일찍 늘 산책을 하곤 했다.

(12) 하얀 집이 전에 언덕 위에 있었다.

(13) 콜럼버스는 미국을 발견하였다.

(14) 그는 12시에 점심을 먹었다.

(15) 그녀는 젊은 시절에 친구가 많았다.

2. 다음 문장을 영작하시오.

(1) He writes a letter in English.

(2) He can write a letter in English.

(3) I would often be absent from school.

(4) It is March 27 today.

(5) My mother would often buy me some apples.

1. 다음 영문을 우리말로 옮기시오.

(1) 나는 내년에 16살이 될 것이다.

(2) 열심히 일하면 당신은 성공할 것이다.

(3) 그녀는 곧 괜찮아질 것이다.

(4) 나는 중국을 알기 위해서 중국어를 배우겠다.

(5) 당신이 가방을 운반하도록 하겠다.

(6) 그가 자동차를 사도록 하겠다.

(7) 저에게 물 한 잔 갖다 주시겠습니까?

(8) 제가 그에게 커피 한 잔을 드릴까요?

(9) 그가 당장 편지를 쓰도록 할까요?

(10) 내일 아침 비가 올까요?

(11) 벌써 그 일을 마쳤습니까?

(12) 나는 그 일을 이미 마쳤다.

(13) 나는 그 일을 아직 마치지 못했다.

(14) 당신은 서울에 얼마나 오래 있었습니까?

(15) 나는 작년부터 계속 서울에 살아왔다.

2. 다음 문장을 영작하시오.

(1) It has been raining for a month.

(2) Will you bring me a glass of milk?

(3) Shall I bring you a cup of coffee?

(4) You will succeed soon.

(5) Have you written a letter yet?

1. 다음 영문을 우리말로 옮기시오.

(1) 당신은 뉴욕에 가본 적이 있습니까?

(2) 나는 뉴욕에 가본 적이 없다.

(3) 나는 뉴욕에 5번 가본 적이 있다.

(4) 나의 아버지는 뉴욕에 가셨습니다. (가시고 안 계십니다.)

(5) 나는 이발소에 갔다 왔다.

(6) 그녀는 지난주부터 계속 앓고 있습니다.

(7) 나는 그 차를 잃어버렸다.

(8) 나는 전에 사자를 본 적이 없었다.

(9) 내가 역에 도착했을 때 기차는 이미 떠나버렸다.

(10) 그는 곧 여기에 올 것이다.

(11) 그녀는 지금 책을 쓰고 있다.

(12) 그는 어제 편지를 쓰고 있었다.

(13) 그녀는 책을 쓰고 있을 것이다.

(14) 나는 이번 주가 되면 다섯 번 그 책을 읽게 될 것이다.

(15) 일주일 동안 비가 계속 내리고 있다.

2. 다음 문장을 영작하시오.

(1) I have been to London.

(2) I have been to Seoul Station to see my father off.

(3) She has gone to America.

(4) He has been ill for a month.

(5) Summer has gone.

종합문제　　　　　　　　　　p.27

1. 다음 (　) 안에서 알맞은 동사형을 고르시오.

(1) take
(2) am taking
(3) goes
(4) went
(5) is
(6) was
(7) arrives
(8) will arrive
(9) is
(10) will arrive
(11) is having
(12) has
(13) is studying
(14) studying
(15) stands

2. 다음 (　) 안에 문장의 시제를 써 넣고 우리말로 옮기시오.

(1) 그녀는 학교에 간다. (현재)

(2) 그녀는 학교에 가고 있다. (현재진행)

(3) 그는 미국에 가버렸다. (현재완료)

(4) 그는 미국에 간 적이 있다. (현재완료)

(5) 오랫동안 비가 오고 있다. (현재완료진행)

(6) 그녀는 10년 동안 서울에서 살아왔다. (현재완료)

(7) 나는 작년부터 계속 앓고 있다. (현재완료)

(8) 나는 어머니가 내게 주셨던 그 시계를 잃어버렸다. (과거완료)

(9) 나는 12시까지 그 일을 끝마칠 것이다. (미래완료)

(10) 나는 그런 음악을 들은 적이 없다. (현재완료)

3. 다음 문장에서 잘못된 곳을 바르게 고치시오.

(1) have you finished → did you finish

(2) shall → will

(3) has arrived → arrived

(4) are you loving → do you love

(5) have gone → have been

(6) has arrived → arrived

(7) lived → have lived

(8) is usually going → usually goes

(9) has done → had done

(10) rained → has been raining

4. 다음 (　) 안에서 알맞은 말을 고르시오.

(1) for
(2) since
(3) wrote
(4) have written
(5) before

5. 다음 (　) 안에서 알맞은 말을 고르시오.

(1) please
(2) I will
(3) let her open it
(4) it will
(5) you will

6. 다음 세 문장의 뜻이 같아지도록 (　) 안에 알맞은 말을 써 넣으시오.

(1) It is
(2) ago

 조동사

연습문제　　　　　　　　　　p.34

1. 다음 영문을 우리말로 옮기시오.

(1) 로마는 하루아침에 만들어지지 않았다.

(2) 그들은 오후에 테니스를 치고 있었다.

(3) 그는 오늘 아침에 서울역에 갔다 왔다.

(4) 그는 영어책을 썼었다.

(5) 나는 어제 공원에서 그녀를 만났다.

(6) 나는 그보다 더 일찍 일어났다.

(7) 나는 음악 듣기를 좋아한다. 그도 그렇다.

(8) 결코 나는 그녀를 다시 만나지 못했다.

(9) 그녀는 영어로 편지를 쓸 수 있을 것이다.

(10) 제가 전화를 사용해도 되나요? 아니오, 안됩니다.

(11) 저에게 물 좀 갖다 주실 수 있습니까?

(12) 그는 의사였을 리가 없다.

(13) 그것은 사실일 리가 없다.

(14) 당신은 자동차를 운전할 때 아무리 조심해도 지나치지 않는다.

(15) 나는 그 우스운 광경을 보고 웃지 않을 수 없었다.

2. 다음 문장을 영작하시오.

(1) Can it be true?

(2) It cannot be true.

(3) Could you lend me your book?

(4) She cannot play the piano. Neither can I.

(5) I cannot but laugh at his red tie.

연습문제   p.38

1. 다음 영문을 우리말로 옮기시오.

(1) 여기서 담배를 피워도 됩니까? 아니오, 안됩니다.

(2) 내일 비가 올까요? 아니오, 안 올지도 모릅니다.

(3) 금년에 눈이 많이 올지도 모릅니다.

(4) 그녀는 부정직했을지도 모릅니다.

(5) 나는 가족을 부양하기 위하여 매우 열심히 일했다.

(6) 당신이 아무리 열심히 노력할지라도 당신은 그 문제를 풀 수가 없다.

(7) 당신이 사업에 성공하는 것은 당연하다.

(8) 당신은 오늘밤에 일찍 잠자리에 드는 것이 좋겠다.

(9) 제가 이 책을 읽어야 합니까? 예, 당신은 이 책을 읽어야 합니다.

(10) 그녀가 오늘 피곤함에 틀림없습니까? 예, 그

녀는 오늘 피곤함에 틀림없습니다.

(11) 오늘 비가 안 올지도 모릅니다.

(12) 그는 의사가 아니었을지도 모릅니다.

(13) 그는 시인이자 선생님임에 틀림없다.

(14) 그녀는 시인이자 과학자였을지도 모릅니다.

(15) 고 링컨 대통령은 국민을 위해서 일했음에 틀림없다.

2. 다음 문장을 영작하시오.

(1) You may read a book here.

(2) We may have snow tomorrow.

(3) Must it be true? Yes, it must be true.

(4) She works hard so that she may succeed.

(5) He must have been a doctor.

연습문제   p.42

1. 다음 영문을 우리말로 옮기시오.

(1) 그녀는 위대한 과학자가 될 것이라고들 했다.

(2) 아버지는 아침에 종종 신문을 읽곤 했다.

(3) 성공하고자 하는 사람들은 열심히 일해야 한다.

(4) 저에게 커피 한 잔 갖다 주시겠습니까?

(5) 나는 그에게 점심을 요리해 주었다. 그러나 그는 먹으려 하지 않았다.

(6) 나는 한가할 때는 음악을 듣고 싶다.

(7) 나는 곧 회복될 것이라고들 했다.

(8) 당신은 그 해에 자동차를 샀어야 했다.

(9) 건강에 주의를 하는 것은 중요하다.

(10) 그는 내가 영어를 공부할 것을 명령했다.

(11) 사람은 누구나 자연을 보호해야 한다.

(12) 당신은 작년에 그 집을 팔지 말았어야 했다.

(13) 그는 늘 버스로 학교에 가곤 했다.

(14) 예전에 호수가 여기에 있었다.

(15) 브라운 씨는 한국 음식을 먹는 데 익숙하다.

2. 다음 문장을 영작하시오.

(1) He would often be asleep in class.

(2) I would like to have a cup of coffee after lunch.

(3) You should not have returned from America.

(4) One should respect one's neighbors.

(5) You need not get up early this morning.

3. 다음 문장을 (   ) 안의 지시대로 바꾸시오.

(1) He will be able to speak Korean.

(2) You will have to study hard.

(3) You had to work hard.

(4) You should not do it.

(5) You ought not to do it.

4. 다음 (   ) 안에 알맞은 말을 써 넣으시오.

(1) may, must(may) (2) must, need
(3) can, can   (4) please, you
(5) will, won't   (6) well
(7) as   (8) let
(9) would   (10) should
(11) might   (12) to
(13) Can, cannot   (14) be
(15) to   (16) could
(17) like   (18) would
(19) to   (20) not
(21) used   (22) used
(23) used

5. 다음 두 문장의 뜻이 같아지도록 (   ) 안에 알맞은 말을 써 넣으시오.

(1) let   (2) to
(3) didn't   (4) met
(5) were   (6) didn't
(7) might   (8) let

6. 다음 영문을 우리말로 옮기시오.

(1) 그녀는 아침에 산책을 하곤 했다.
(2) 그녀는 숙제를 했어야만 했다.
(3) 전에 언덕 위에 작은 집 한 채가 있었다.
(4) 그가 혼자의 힘으로 숙제를 한다는 것은 당연하다.
(5) 나는 테니스를 치는 데 익숙하다.
(6) 나의 친구는 매우 행복함에 틀림없다.
(7) 성공을 하고자 하는 사람은 열심히 일해야 한다.
(8) 당신은 밤에 피아노를 쳐서는 안 된다.
(9) 나는 첫 기차를 놓치지 않기 위해서 일찍 일어났다.
(10) 제가 창문을 열까요?

종합문제   p.45

1. 다음 (   ) 안에서 알맞은 말을 고르시오.

(1) should   (2) Would
(3) would   (4) should
(5) would   (6) will
(7) shall   (8) Will
(9) Shall   (10) Shall

2. 다음 문장에서 잘못된 곳을 바르게 고치시오.

(1) ought to not → ought not to
(2) did he went → did he go
(3) will can → will be able to
(4) used to eat → used to eating
(5) should not → should
(6) should → could
(7) to seeing → to see
(8) must not → need not
(9) must not → cannot
(10) may → might

PART 03 부정사

연습문제   p.54

1. 다음 문장에 쓰인 부정사의 용법을 (   ) 안에 써 넣고 우리말로 옮기시오.

(1) 영어를 배우는 것은 흥미 있다. (명사적 용법－주어)
(2) 나는 런던에 가기를 원한다. (명사적 용법－목적어)
(3) 나의 희망은 여름에 수영을 하는 것이다. (명사적 용법－보어)
(4) 엄마, 저에게 먹을 것을 좀 주세요. (형용사적 용법－명사 수식)
(5) 그는 공부를 하기 위해 학교에 갔다. (부사적 용법 －목적)
(6) 나는 그 소식을 듣고 깜짝 놀랐다. (부사적 용법－원인)
(7) 그녀가 그런 질문에 대답하다니 영리함에 틀림없다. (부사적 용법－이유)
(8) 그는 자라서 위대한 시인이 되었다. (부사적

용법–결과)

(9) 소풍을 간다면 나는 행복할 텐데. (부사적 용
법–조건)

(10) 이 책은 읽기 어렵다. (부사적 용법–형용사
수식)

(11) 이 책은 너무 어려워서 그가 읽을 수 없다. (
부사적 용법–부사 수식)

(12) 이 책은 그가 읽을 만큼 충분히 쉽다. (부사적
용법–부사 수식)

(13) 사실을 말하면 그는 정직하지 않다. (부사적
용법–독립 부사)

(14) 중국어를 배우는 것은 재미있다. (명사적 용
법–주어)

(15) 그녀는 내일 집에 갈 것이다. (형용사적 용
법–예정)

2. 다음 문장을 영작하시오.

(1) I want to read a book.

(2) I go to school to study.

(3) He has no house to live in.

(4) She is happy to meet her friend.

(5) It is important to study hard.

연습문제　　　　　　　　　　　　p.58

1. 다음 영문을 우리말로 옮기시오.

(1) 나는 아침 일찍 일어나기를 원한다.

(2) 나는 그가 아침 일찍 일어나기를 원한다.

(3) 나는 학교에 늦지 않기를 원한다.

(4) 그는 나에게 일찍 잠자리에 들라고 말했다.

(5) 그는 나에게 파티에 올 것을 요청했다.

(6) 그녀는 그에게 편지 쓸 것을 약속했다.

(7) 나는 그녀가 일요일에 교회에 가는 것을 보았
다.

(8) 나는 그녀가 일요일에 교회에 가고 있는 것을
보았다.

(9) 나는 그녀에게 방을 청소하도록 시켰다.

(10) 나는 그에게 가방을 운반하도록 시켰다.

(11) 당신의 이름을 알려 주세요.

(12) 영어로 편지를 쓰는 것은 어렵다.

(13) 그가 영어로 편지를 쓰는 것은 어렵다.

(14) 네가 그렇게 말하다니 친절하다.

(15) 나는 이 책을 읽는 것이 어렵다는 것을 알았다.

2. 다음 문장을 영작하시오.

(1) I want to study English hard.

(2) I want you to study English hard.

(3) I told her to open the window.

(4) I saw him writing a letter.

(5) It is not easy for him to study English.

연습문제　　　　　　　　　　　　p.62

1. 다음 단문을 복문으로 만드시오.

(1) It seems that he is poor.

(2) It seemed that she was sick.

(3) It seems that he was poor.

(4) It seemed that she had been sick.

(5) It is said that she is honest.

(6) It is believed that she was a doctor.

(7) I wish that I shall be happy.

(8) I expect that I shall succeed.

(9) I expect that he will succeed.

(10) He is so old that he can not go to the
mountain by himself.

(11) She is so kind that she can tell me the way
to the station.

(12) She got up early so that she might catch the
first train.

(13) He studied English hard so that he might
pass the examination.

(14) He studied hard so that he might not fail in
the examination.

(15) I have no friend that I can play with.

(16) He is the first Korean that flew across the
Pacific.

(17) I don't know what I should do next.

(18) Do you know where you should go?

(19) This book is so difficult that he cannot read
it.

(20) It is natural that she should say so.

2. 다음 두 문장의 뜻이 같아지도록 (　) 안에 알맞은 말
을 써 넣으시오.

(1) should (2) to

(3) so, cannot (4) so, can

(5) for (6) to

(7) for, him, to   (8) to

(9) to   (10) who

(11) she, is   (12) will

(13) is   (14) was

(15) was   (16) had, bought

(17) he, is   (18) would

종합문제   p.65

1. 다음 ( ) 안에 알맞은 말을 써 넣으시오.

(1) for   (2) of

(3) it   (4) to

(5) to   (6) It

(7) too   (8) as

(9) might   (10) to

2. 다음 ( ) 안에 알맞은 말을 골라 넣으시오.

(1) ①   (2) ③

(3) ②   (4) ①

(5) ②

3. 다음 문장에서 잘못된 곳이 있으면 바르게 고치시오.

(1) to sing → sing

(2) going → to go

(3) that she is going → her to go

(4) She is impossible to do the work. → It is impossible for her to do the work.

 동명사

연습문제   p.73

1. 다음 영문을 우리말로 옮기시오.

(1) 많은 책을 읽는 것은 모든 사람에게 좋다.

(2) 나는 가을에 많은 책 읽기를 즐긴다.

(3) 나의 취미는 책을 읽는 것이다.

(4) 나는 일요일에 낚시하러 가기를 좋아한다.

(5) 나는 그가 시험에 합격하리라 확신한다.

(6) 나는 당신이 매우 열심히 공부할 것을 주장했다.

(7) 그녀는 자기 아들이 과학자인 것을 자랑으로 여긴다.

(8) 그녀는 밤에 외출하는 것을 두려워했다.

(9) 보는 것이 믿는 것이다.

(10) 나는 그가 시험에 합격하기를 원한다.

(11) 나는 그가 시험에 합격하리라 확신했다.

(12) 나는 그가 시험에 합격하리라 확신한다.

(13) 나는 그가 시험에 합격했던 것을 자랑으로 여긴다.

(14) 나는 그가 시험에 합격했었던 것을 자랑으로 여겼다.

(15) 나는 침대차에서 자고 있는 아기를 안다.

2. 다음 문장을 영작하시오.

(1) I am fond of swimming in summer.

(2) I want him to swim.

(3) I am sure of his swimming well.

(4) My hobby is skating in winter.

(5) I am proud of having been a doctor.

연습문제   p.77

1. 다음 영문을 우리말로 옮기시오.

(1) 나는 가을에 책 읽기를 원한다.

(2) 나는 책 읽기를 마쳤다.

(3) 나는 그녀에게 약간의 꽃을 보냈던 것을 기억했다.

(4) 나는 그녀에게 꽃을 보내야 할 것을 기억했다.

(5) 나는 중국어를 배워 보았다.

(6) 나는 중국어를 배우려고 노력했다.

(7) 나는 지난주에 담배를 끊었다.

(8) 나는 담배를 피우려고 정지했다.

(9) 나는 작년 여름에 강에 낚시하러 갔다.

(10) 그는 자기 자동차를 세차하느라고 바쁘다.

(11) 비 때문에 나는 파티에 가지 못했다.

(12) 나는 열심히 일하지 않을 수 없다.

(13) 나를 보자마자 그는 도망쳤다.

(14) 문을 좀 열어 주시겠습니까?

(15) 내가 너를 볼 때마다 나의 형 생각이 난다.

2. 다음 문장을 영작하시오.

(1) I went shopping to the supermarket with my mother.

(2) I forgot to meet my friend at the party yesterday.

(3) My mother is busy cooking in the kitchen.

(4) She finished writing a letter.

(5) She began learning Chinese. or She began to learn Chinese.

3. 다음 (   ) 안에서 알맞은 말을 고르시오.

(1) reading (2) to read

(3) seeing (4) to see

(5) to swim or swimming

(6) playing (7) meeting

(8) collecting or to collect

(9) want (10) hope

4. 다음 두 문장이 뜻이 같아지도록 (   ) 안에 알맞은 말을 써 넣으시오.

(1) Getting (2) was

(3) for (4) learning

(5) I, shall (6) I, should

(7) he, is (8) he, was

(9) saw (10) will

종합문제 p.79

1. 다음 두 문장이 뜻이 같아지도록 (   ) 안에 알맞은 말을 써 넣으시오.

(1) As, soon, as (2) but

(3) Whenever (4) needless

(5) about (6) Let's

(7) Because (8) I, should

(9) impossible (10) never

2. 다음 문장에서 잘못된 곳이 있으면 바르게 고치시오.

(1) going → to go

(2) 없음

(3) to go → going

(4) go → going

(5) that → this

3. 다음 문장을 밑줄 친 부분에 유의하여 우리말로 옮기시오.

(1) 나는 그것을 만들려고 시도했다.

(2) 나는 그것을 만들려고 노력했다.

(3) 나는 담배를 끊었다.

(4) 나는 담배를 피우려고 정지했다.

PART 05 분사

연습문제 p.86

1. 다음 영문을 우리말로 옮기시오.

(1) 나는 울고 있는 아기를 만났다.

(2) 나는 방에서 울고 있는 한 아기를 안다.

(3) 나는 부서진 창문을 발견했다.

(4) 나는 어느 시인에 의해 쓰여진 책을 샀다.

(5) 나는 앉아서 신문을 읽고 있었다.

(6) 나는 아이들에게 둘러싸인 채 앉아 있었다.

(7) 나는 그가 편지를 쓰고 있는 것을 보았다.

(8) 나는 그가 편지 쓰는 것을 보았다.

(9) 그 건물은 한국인들에 의해 건축되었다.

(10) 그녀는 미국에 간 적이 있다.

(11) 그녀는 미국에 가버렸다.

(12) 나는 시계를 도난당했다.

(13) 나는 라디오를 수선시켰다.

(14) 나는 내 말을 영어로 이해시킬 수 없다.

(15) 나는 그녀가 노래하고 있는 것을 들었다.

2. 다음 문장을 영작하시오.

(1) The baby sleeping in the room is my brother.

(2) I saw a sleeping baby.

(3) He came crying.

(4) I saw her running.

(5) I saw her run.

3. 다음 (   ) 안에서 알맞은 말을 고르시오.

(1) sleeping (2) killed

(3) excited (4) exciting

(5) writing (6) exhausted

(7) built (8) to learn

(9) finished (10) reading

(11) surrounded (12) looking

(13) known (14) make

(15) to make (16) taken

(17) cut (18) understood

(19) waiting (20) closed

4. 다음 ( ) 안의 동사를 알맞은 꼴로 바꾸시오.

(1) spoken   (2) running

(3) lighted   (4) burning

(5) interesting

연습문제   p.93

1. 다음 영문을 우리말로 옮기시오.

(1) 신문을 읽고 있었을 때 나는 친구의 방문을 받았다.

(2) 아침 식사를 한 후에 나는 버스로 학교에 갔다.

(3) 피곤하므로 나는 오늘밤 일찍 잠자리에 들고 싶다.

(4) 기차가 이미 떠났기 때문에 나는 회의에 갈 수 없었다.

(5) 일찍 일어나면 당신은 첫 기차를 탈 수 있다.

(6) 그의 집 근처에 살지만 나는 그를 모른다.

(7) 나는 음악을 들으면서 책을 읽고 있다.

(8) 쉽게 쓰였으므로 그 책은 모두에게 읽힌다.

(9) 일반적으로 말하면 그는 세계에서 위대한 사람이다.

(10) 오늘은 날씨가 좋으므로 나는 밖으로 나가고 싶다.

(11) 길을 걷고 있는 동안 나는 소녀를 만났다.

(12) 읽히지 않으므로 그 책은 잘 팔리지 않았다.

(13) 그녀에게 편지를 쓰지 않아서 나는 매우 미안했다.

(14) 그의 집 근처에 살고는 있지만 나는 그를 모른다.

(15) 태양이 떴으므로 나는 전등을 껐다.

2. 다음 문장을 영작하시오.

(1) Being tired, I want to stay at home today.

(2) It being fine today, he wants to go on a picnic.

(3) Having had dinner, I watched television.

(4) Seeing him, she ran away.

(5) Walking along the street, I met her.

3. 다음 두 문장의 뜻이 같아지도록 ( ) 안에 알맞은 말을 써 넣으시오.

(1) Walking   (2) Not, knowing

(3) Turning   (4) Being

(5) Generally, speaking   (6) It, being

(7) Having, breakfasted   (8) Having

(9) Written   (10) The, book, written

(11) smiling   (12) arriving

(13) As, I, was   (14) As, I, am

(15) As, I, had, been   (16) As, it, is

종합문제   p.95

1. 다음 복문을 단문으로 고치시오.

(1) Seeing a police officer, he ran away.

(2) Having had dinner, he watched TV and listened to music.

(3) Being poor, she can not go to college.

(4) Being poor, she could not go to college.

(5) It being fine today, I want to go to the mountain.

(6) Having been a doctor, he can solve the problem.

(7) Turning to the right, you will find the building.

(8) Being poor, he was honest.

(9) I arrived in New York at seven, staying there for a week.

(10) Smiling brightly, she shook hands with me.

2. 다음 단문을 복문으로 고치시오.

(1) As I am busy, I cannot go to your birthday party.

(2) As I was busy, I could not go to the meeting.

(3) As I have been ill, I can not walk for a long time.

(4) As he has no money, he can not buy that car.

(5) If it is fine today, I will go out.

(6) Though I live near his house, I don't know him.

(7) If we speak generally, she is a good doctor.

(8) If you turn to the left, you will find the building.

(9) As the book is written in English, it is difficult to read.

(10) As the book had been written in English, it was difficult.

연습문제   p.106

1. 다음 영문을 우리말로 옮기시오.
   (1) 그녀는 그에 의해 사랑을 받는다.
   (2) 많은 희곡이 셰익스피어에 의해 쓰여졌다.
   (3) 신문이 아버지에 의해 읽혀지고 있다.
   (4) 그녀는 그에 의해 행복해졌다.
   (5) 그가 영어를 잘한다고 한다.
   (6) 한라산은 눈으로 덮여 있다.
   (7) 그 일을 빨리 마쳐지도록 하지 마라.
   (8) 그 집은 언제 팔렸습니까?
   (9) 그 책은 누구에 의해 쓰여졌습니까?
   (10) 그는 과학에 흥미가 있다.
   (11) 그 소설은 모두에게 알려져 있다.
   (12) 그녀가 산에 올라가는 것이 보였다.
   (13) 포도주는 포도로 만들어진다.
   (14) 나는 영어를 공부하는 데 싫증이 나지 않는다.
   (15) 나는 그 소식을 듣고 깜짝 놀랐다.

2. 다음 문장을 영작하시오.
   (1) A rat was caught by a cat.
   (2) I am loved by my teacher.
   (3) The book was not written by him.
   (4) English is spoken in Canada.
   (5) Many apples are filled in the box. (=The box is filled with many apples.)

3. 다음 (   ) 안에서 알맞은 말을 고르시오.
   (1) his   (2) him
   (3) with   (4) of
   (5) of   (6) from
   (7) to   (8) by
   (9) with   (10) by

4. 다음 두 문장의 뜻이 같아지도록 (   ) 안에 알맞은 말을 써 넣으시오.

(1) being   (2) been
(3) be   (4) were
(5) was   (6) made
(7) By, whom   (8) was, wanted
(9) to   (10) Was

5. 다음 문장을 수동태로 고치시오.
   (1) A book is written by him.
   (2) The work was finished by Tom.
   (3) A book is being written by him.
   (4) His homework has been finished by Tom.
   (5) It was given (to) me by her.
   (6) He was seen to read many books by me.
   (7) I was made to carry the box by her.
   (8) A box was made to me by him.
   (9) A letter was written to me by him.
   (10) It was said that the earth is round.
   (11) English is spoken in Canada.
   (12) I was surprised at the news.
   (13) I was laughed at by them.
   (14) Her baby is taken care of by her.
   (15) Let the work be done quickly.
   (16) Was a model airplane made by him?
   (17) Where is a handbag bought by her?
   (18) By whom was America discovered?
   (19) What was wanted by him?
   (20) A kangaroo was never seen by her.

종합문제   p.109

1. 다음 (   ) 안에 알맞은 말을 써 넣으시오.
   (1) by   (2) in
   (3) to   (4) with
   (5) with or at

2. 다음 문장을 능동태로 고치시오.
   (1) She loved him.
   (2) Did Columbus discover America?
   (3) When did he buy a car?
   (4) Who broke the window?
   (5) I saw him read a book.

3. 다음 문장에서 잘못된 곳을 바르게 고치시오.

(1) repair → repaired
(2) repaired → repair
(3) did → was
(4) with → in
(5) enter → to enter

4. 다음 ( ) 안에 알맞은 말을 써 넣으시오.

(1) was, was
(2) believed, had, been, believed, to
(3) be, not, be

 가정법

연습문제   p.115

1. 다음 영문을 우리말로 옮기시오.

(1) 너는 오늘 아침에 늦지 않는 것이 좋겠다.
(2) 너는 왜 어제 학교에 지각했니?
(3) 당신은 아침에 언제 일어납니까?
(4) 나는 당신이 아침에 언제 일어나는지 모른다.
(5) 당신은 아프지요, 그렇지 않아요?
(6) 그는 어제 집에 있었습니까?
(7) 이 도시는 참 아름답군요!
(8) 파티에 갑시다.
(9) 우리를 파티에 가도록 해주세요.
(10) 그녀에게 영어를 열심히 공부하게 하십시오.
(11) 열심히 공부해라, 그러면 너는 시험에 합격할 것이다.
(12) 집에 일찍 가라, 그렇지 않으면 너는 집에 갈 수 없다.
(13) 밤에 너무 늦게 밖에 나가지 마라.
(14) 그녀를 밤에 혼자서 밖에 나가지 못하도록 하라.
(15) 딩신이 그녀의 생일 파티에 간다면, 당신은 행복할 것이다.

2. 다음 문장을 영작하시오.

(1) Where do you live now?
(2) Do you know where he lives?
(3) How nice this car is!
(4) Let's go home early.
(5) Don't go out too late at night.

연습문제   p.121

1. 다음 영문을 우리말로 옮기시오.

(1) 만일 그가 정직하다면, 나는 그를 좋아할 텐데.
(2) 만일 그가 정직했더라면, 나는 그를 좋아했을 텐데.
(3) 만일 내가 많은 돈이 있다면, 나는 멋진 자동차를 살 수 있을 텐데.
(4) 만일 내가 많은 돈이 있었더라면, 나는 멋진 자동차를 살 수 있었을 텐데.
(5) 혹시라도 내일 비가 오면, 나는 회의에 가지 않을 것이다.
(6) 내가 젊으면 좋을 텐데.
(7) 내가 다시 소년이 된다면, 매우 열심히 공부할 텐데.
(8) 그녀는 자기가 마치 의사인 것처럼 말한다.
(9) 당신의 도움이 없다면, 나는 성공하지 못할 텐데.
(10) 당신이 열심히 일하지 않는다면, 당신은 성공하지 못할 것이다.
(11) 물이 없다면, 지구상에 아무것도 살 수 없을 텐데.
(12) 태양이 없었더라면, 우리는 더 이상 살 수 없었을 텐데.
(13) 내가 모든 것을 알았더라면 좋을 텐데.
(14) 그녀는 자기가 모든 것을 알았던 것처럼 말했다.
(15) 그녀를 다시 만나면 나는 행복할 텐데.

2. 다음 문장을 영작하시오.

(1) I wish I were rich.
(2) If I were a bird, I would fly to you.
(3) He talks as if he were a scientist.
(4) If she had been poor, she could not have gone to college.
(5) But for my uncle's help, I should not have succeeded.

3. 다음 ( ) 안에서 알맞은 말을 고르시오.

(1) were   (2) have bought
(3) buy   (4) should
(5) is

4. 다음 ( ) 안에 알맞은 말을 써 넣으시오.

(1) and
(2) or
(3) to
(4) How
(5) Let
(6) were
(7) for
(8) were
(9) had
(10) should

5. 다음 두 문장의 뜻이 같아지도록 ( ) 안에 알맞을 말을 써 넣으시오.

(1) But, for
(2) Without
(3) As, don't, can't
(4) As, didn't, couldn't
(5) am, not

종합문제　　　　　　　　　　p.123

1. 다음 두 문장의 뜻이 같아지도록 밑줄 친 곳에 알맞은 말을 써 넣으시오.

(1) I am not rich, I cannot go to college.
(2) I was not rich, I could not study more.
(3) am sorry I cannot speak English well.
(4) am sorry I could not speak English well.
(5) it were not for the sun, we could not live.
(6) it had not been for the sun, we could not have lived.
(7) he doesn't have a beautiful girl friend, he is not happy.
(8) I had much money, I bought a nice car.

2. 다음 문장에서 잘못된 곳이 있으면 바르게 고치시오.

(1) was → were
(2) have bought → buy
(3) it will → it should
(4) was → were
(5) Without → But
(6) or → and
(7) help → have helped

PART
08 화법

연습문제　　　　　　　　　　p.131

1. 다음 영문을 우리말로 옮기시오.

(1) 그와 당신 중에서 한 사람은 잘못이다.
(2) 그와 나 중에서 아무도 잘못이 없다.
(3) 로미오와 줄리엣은 셰익스피어에 의해 쓰여진 유명한 희곡이다.
(4) 나는 영어뿐만 아니라 불어도 말할 수 있다.
(5) 나는 영어는 물론 불어도 말할 수 있다.
(6) 나의 학급은 큰 학급이다.
(7) 나의 학급의 학생들은 모두 부지런하다.
(8) 모든 소년과 소녀는 영어를 배우고 있다.
(9) 각 소년과 소녀는 책상을 가지고 있다.
(10) 수학은 우리가 공부하기에 어렵다.
(11) 그녀는 내가 정직하다고 믿는다.
(12) 그녀는 내가 정직하다고 믿었다.
(13) 그는 태양이 달보다 더 크다고 믿었다.
(14) 당신은 누가 라디오를 발명했는지 아십니까?
(15) 그는 그녀가 매일 아침에 산책을 한다고 말했다.

2. 다음 문장을 영작하시오.

(1) My family are all busy.
(2) Either you or I am wrong.
(3) He thinks that she is honest.
(4) He thought that she was honest.
(5) Not only you but also he is handsome.

연습문제　　　　　　　　　　p.138

1. 다음 영문을 우리말로 옮기시오.

(1) 그녀는 "나는 행복하다."라고 말했다.
(2) 그녀는 자기가 행복하다고 말했다.
(3) 그는 "내가 당신을 좋아한다."라고 나에게 말했다.
(4) 그는 자기가 나를 좋아한다고 나에게 말했다.
(5) 그는 "내가 어제 이 책을 그녀에게 주었다."라고 나에게 말했다.
(6) 그는 자기가 그 전날 그 책을 그녀에게 주었다고 나에게 말했다.
(7) 그녀는 "당신은 책을 읽고 있습니까?"라고 나에게 말했다.
(8) 그녀는 내가 책을 읽고 있었느냐고 나에게 물었다.
(9) 그는 "너는 2주 전에 학교를 결석했니?"라고

나에게 말했다.

(10) 그는 내가 2주 전에 학교에 결석했었는지 나에게 물었다.

(11) 그녀는 "당신은 무엇을 원합니까?"라고 나에게 말했다.

(12) 그녀는 내가 무엇을 원하는지 나에게 물었다.

(13) 그는 "빨리 학교에 가라."라고 나에게 말했다.

(14) 그는 빨리 학교에 가라고 나에게 말했다.

(15) 그녀는 "서울은 참 아름답구나!"라고 말했다.

(16) 그녀는 서울은 참 아름답다고 소리쳤다.

2. 다음 문장을 영작하시오.

(1) She told me to study English hard.

(2) She asked me where I lived.

(3) He asked me what she was doing.

(4) He told me not to go home late.

3. 다음 ( ) 안에서 알맞은 말을 고르시오.

(1) are   (2) am

(3) am   (4) is

(5) am   (6) am

(7) is   (8) are

(9) is   (10) has

(11) is   (12) was

(13) is   (14) is

(15) was   (16) had been

(17) is   (18) goes

(19) discovered   (20) asked

(21) was   (22) how

(23) that

4. 다음 두 문장의 뜻이 같아지도록 ( ) 안에 알맞은 말을 써 넣으시오.

(1) was, then

(2) had, given

(3) would, there, the, next, day

(4) if, I

(5) what, I

(6) who, had

(7) to

(8) suggested, that

(9) cried, out, how

(10) said, that

5. 다음 문장에서 잘못된 곳이 있으면 바르게 고치시오.

(1) takes a bath → 그대로

(2) saw → had seen

(3) is → was

(4) to not → not to

(5) studies → studied

(6) did I study → I studied

(7) is → was

(8) had discovered → discovered

종합문제   p.141

1. 다음 문장을 간접화법으로 고치시오.

(1) She said that she was very happy there.

(2) She told me that she had given me that book the day before.

(3) He asked me if I was busy then.

(4) He asked me if he was reading a book.

(5) She asked me what I wanted to do.

(6) She asked me who had invented the radio.

(7) He asked me where she had bought the car the week before.

(8) He told me to study English hard.

(9) She told me not to be late that night.

(10) She asked me to close the door.

(11) He suggested that we should have lunch at twelve.

(12) He cried out how tall that building was.

(13) She prayed that God might bless me.

(14) He said that she was very kind and he wanted to meet her.

(15) The doctor advised me not to smoke too much for my health.

2. 다음 문장을 직접화법으로 고치시오.

(1) He said to me, "I was a pilot."

(2) She said to me, "Be kind to others."

(3) He said to me, "Will you get up early in the morning?"

(4) She said to me, "When did you buy this car?"

(5) He said, "I am happy now."

연습문제   p.148

1. 다음 영문을 우리말로 옮기시오.

(1) 톰과 잭은 형제이다.

(2) 톰, 잭, 그리고 토미는 나의 동급생이다.

(3) 당신은 커피와 우유 중에서 어느 것을 더 좋아 합니까?

(4) 지금 당장 나를 보러 와라.

(5) 하려고 노력하라, 그러면 당신은 무엇이든지 할 것이다.

(6) 친구를 사귀어라, 그렇지 않으면 너는 불행할 것이다.

(7) 나는 지난밤에 감기에 걸렸다, 왜냐하면 나는 찬 방에서 잤기 때문이다.

(8) 그뿐만 아니라 당신도 훌륭한 선생님이다.

(9) 그는 물론 당신도 훌륭한 선생님이다.

(10) 나는 톰과 메리 둘 다 좋아한다.

(11) 그녀와 나 중에서 하나는 행복하다.

(12) 그녀와 나 중에서 어느 누구도 행복하지 않다.

(13) 나는 바빠서 당신의 생일 파티에 갈 수 없다.

(14) 나는 바빴다, 그래서 나는 당신의 생일 파티 에 갈 수 없었다.

(15) 그녀는 여름과 겨울 중에서 하나도 좋아하지 않는다.

2. 다음 문장을 영작하시오.

(1) Work hard, and you will succeed.

(2) Be a good man, or they will not like you.

(3) Come and see me tonight.

(4) I can speak not only Japanese but also Chinese.

(5) Neither Tom nor Jack is wrong.

연습문제   p.154

1. 다음 영문을 우리말로 옮기시오.

(1) 저는 아버지가 제 생일날에 저에게 주셨던 똑 같은 시계를 잃어버렸습니다.

(2) 나는 그가 위대한 음악가였다는 사실을 안다.

(3) 나는 그녀가 유명한 시인이라고 생각했다.

(4) 그녀가 과학자라는 것은 확실하다.

(5) 이것은 내가 며칠 전에 산 똑같은 자동차이다.

(6) 네가 무엇을 하고 싶은지 나에게 말해 달라.

(7) 당신이 가지고 싶은 것 무엇이든지 나에게 말 해 줄 수 있습니까?

(8) 나는 그녀를 처음 만났던 그 장소를 기억할 수 없다.

(9) 당신이 태어난 장소를 나에게 말해 주십시오.

(10) 내가 신문을 읽고 있는 동안 나의 남동생은 TV를 보았다.

(11) 나는 바빠서 회의에 참석할 수 없었다.

(12) 그는 피곤해서 쉬기를 원한다.

(13) 그는 그녀가 어디를 가든 간에 그녀를 그리워 할 것이다.

(14) 그녀는 코트를 입었다, 왜냐하면 너무 추웠기 때문이었다.

(15) 우리는 추워서 불을 피웠다.

2. 다음 문장을 영작하시오.

(1) I studied hard when I was young.

(2) Wherever you may go, you will not forget me.

(3) If it is fine tomorrow, I will stay here.

(4) I want to have what he has.

(5) As she is tired, she wants to go to bed.

연습문제   p.156

1. 다음 영문을 우리말로 옮기시오.

(1) 당신이 부지런하지 않다면 당신은 성공하지 못 할 것이다.

(2) 그는 약하지만 매일 열심히 공부한다.

(3) 그녀는 젊지만 많은 경험을 가지고 있다.

(4) 나는 그들에게 영어를 가르치기 위해서 6시에 여기에 도착했다.

(5) 나는 학교에 늦지 않으려고 서둘렀다.

(6) 이 책은 너무 어려워서 나는 그것을 읽을 수 없 다.

(7) 이것은 좋은 책이어서 우리는 그것을 읽어야 한다.

(8) 이 학교는 저 학교보다 더 크다.

(9) 이 학교는 저 학교만큼 크다.

(10) 그는 자기가 마치 선생님인 것처럼 말한다.

(11) 그들은 중국까지 여행했다.

(12) 그녀는 나를 보자 도망쳤다.

(13) 그녀가 나를 보자 도망쳤다.

(14) 당신이 아무리 열심히 일하더라도 당신은 성공할 수 없다.

(15) 당신이 무엇을 갖기를 원하든 간에 나는 당신에게 모든 것을 주겠다.

2. 다음 문장을 영작하시오.

(1) If you love me, I will love you.

(2) She is so diligent that she is loved by everyone.

(3) She is not so beautiful as my mother.

(4) I got up early lest I should be late for school.

(5) As soon as I got up, I brushed my teeth and washed my face.

3. 다음 ( ) 안에서 알맞은 말을 고르시오.

(1) and   (2) but

(3) and   (4) or

(5) Because   (6) nor

(7) that   (8) if

(9) that   (10) As

(11) than   (12) If

(13) whether   (14) during

(15) while

4. 다음 ( ) 안에 알맞은 말을 써 넣으시오.

(1) or   (2) what

(3) as   (4) that

(5) might   (6) should

(7) if   (8) may

(9) so   (10) such

종합문제   p.158

1. 다음 두 문장의 뜻이 같아지도록 ( ) 안에 알맞은 말을 써 넣으시오.

(1) so   (2) as, well, as

(3) neither, nor   (4) if

(5) Unless   (6) lest, should

(7) As, soon, as   (8) In

(9) to   (10) However

2. 다음 문장의 밑줄 친 부분의 뜻을 구별하여 우리말로 옮기시오.

(1) 그는 성공하기 위해서 열심히 일했다.

(2) 그는 열심히 일해서 그는 성공할 수 있었다.

(3) 그는 열심히 일했다, 그 결과 그는 성공했다.

(4) 그녀와 나 중에서 하나는 잘못이다.

(5) 그녀와 나 중에서 아무도 잘못이 없다.

(6) 열심히 일하라, 그렇지 않으면 당신은 실패할 것이다.

(7) 열심히 일하라, 그러면 당신은 성공할 것이다.

(8) 나는 그녀가 곧 올지 안 올지 모르겠다.

PART 10 문장 전환

연습문제   p.166

1. 다음 영문을 우리말로 옮기시오.

(1) 일찍 일어나라, 그러면 너는 첫 버스를 탈 수 있을 것이다.

(2) 일찍 일어나라, 그렇지 않으면 너는 학교에 늦을 것이다.

(3) 그는 피곤하다, 그러나 그는 그 일을 마쳐야 한다.

(4) 바쁘지만 나는 달마다 어머니에게 편지를 썼다.

(5) 나의 친구는 아파서 나와 같이 산에 갈 수 없었다.

(6) 그녀는 1주일 동안 앓았다, 그래서 그녀는 일을 계속할 수 없다.

(7) 만일 당신이 많은 책을 읽지 않는다면, 당신은 많은 지식을 얻지 못할 것이다.

(8) 당신이 열심히 공부하지 않는다면, 당신은 대학에 들어갈 수 없다.

(9) 당신이 어디를 가든 간에, 당신우 환영을 받을 것이다.

(10) 나는 성공하기를 희망했지만, 성공하지 못했다.

(11) 그녀는 아주 열심히 일했지만 결국 사업에 실패를 했다.

(12) 특급열차는 6시에 서울서 떠나 11시에 부산에 도착한다.

(13) 나는 그를 좋아하지 않는다, 왜냐하면 그는 게으르고 부정직하기 때문이다.

(14) 그녀는 나이가 많지만 그런 일을 할 수 있다.

(15) 그는 시를 쓸 뿐만 아니라 자동차도 판다.

2. 다음 문장을 영작하시오.

(1) Be diligent, and you will succeed.

(2) Try to finish the work, or you will be unhappy.

(3) As I was tired yesterday, I went to bed early.

(4) Though I am busy, I will go to see you.

(5) If it is rainy tomorrow, I will stay at home.

3. 다음 중문을 복문으로 바꾸시오.

(1) Though she lives near my house, she doesn't know me.

(2) As he studied hard, he passed the examination.

(3) If you get up early, you will not be late for school.

(4) If you are late for school, you will be punished by your teacher.

(5) After he finished the work, he went to the movies.

(6) As she is very busy, she cannot go to the party.

4. 다음 중문을 단문으로 바꾸시오.

(1) His father being very rich, he can go abroad to study more.

(2) The train leaves Incheon at six, arriving in Seoul at ten.

(3) He grew up to be a pilot.

(4) She worked hard only to fail in the business.

(5) In spite of her excitement, she kept her temper.

(6) Besides teaching English, he writes English books.

(7) I hoped to have met her.

(8) He was absent from school because of his illness.

(9) Having no house to live in, I am unhappy.

(10) His brother is too young to go to school.

(11) Without working hard, you will fail in life.

(12) The English book was written easy enough to be sold well.

(13) Knowing is quite different from teaching.

(14) I am too poor to help them.

연습문제   p.173

1. 다음 영문을 우리말로 옮기시오.

(1) 나는 그가 정직하다고 믿는다.

(2) 나는 그가 부정직했다고 생각한다.

(3) 나는 성공하리라 기대한다.

(4) 나는 성공하리라 기대했다.

(5) 나는 시험에 합격하기를 희망했으나 합격 못했다.

(6) 그녀는 의사라고 했다.

(7) 그녀가 책을 쓰는 것은 불가능하다.

(8) 나는 그 책을 읽는 것이 쉽다고 생각한다.

(9) 그녀는 자기 아들이 의사인 것을 자랑스럽게 여긴다.

(10) 나는 어디에 가야 할지 모른다.

(11) 나는 그가 영어 배우기를 원한다.

(12) 나는 그의 결백을 믿는다.

(13) 나는 그의 출생지를 모른다.

(14) 그녀가 그런 일을 하는 것은 놀랍다.

(15) 나는 한 달에 책 한 권을 쓰는 것이 불가능하다는 것을 알았다.

2. 다음 문장을 영작하시오

(1) I want him to succeed.

(2) I am sure of his success.

(3) I think it difficult to learn English.

(4) I don't know what to do next.

(5) It is impossible for her to read a book a week.

3. 다음 단문을 복문으로 바꾸시오.

(1) I expect that I shall succeed.

(2) I expect that he will succeed.

(3) I expected that I should succeed.

(4) I expected that he would succeed.

(5) I think that she is honest.

(6) It is said that she is honest.

(7) It was said that she was honest.

(8) It is believed that he was diligent.

(9) It was believed that he had been diligent.

(10) I am sure that she will be wise.

(11) I found that it is right to do so.

(12) It is impossible that she should speak Korean.

(13) I don't know what I should do next.

(14) I doubt that his statement is true.

(15) I am sure that he will succeed.

(16) I don't know the place where she was born.

(17) I insisted that he should study English hard.

(18) It is strange that she should say so.

(19) She is proud that her son is a doctor.

(20) She is proud that her son was a doctor.

연습문제 p.181

1. 다음 영문을 우리말로 옮기시오.

(1) 그는 태평양을 비행 횡단한 최초의 한국인이다.

(2) 이것은 내가 읽어야 하는 책이다.

(3) 그는 중요한 사람이다.

(4) 나는 회의에 늦지 않으려고 일찍 일어났다.

(5) 이 책은 너무 어려워서 그녀는 읽을 수 없다.

(6) 이 책은 그녀가 읽을 만큼 쉽다.

(7) 그는 첫 버스를 타려고 일찍 일어났다.

(8) 그는 일찍 일어나서 첫 버스를 탔다.

(9) 그녀의 친구를 만나서 그녀는 매우 행복했다.

(10) 부지런하기 때문에 그녀는 성공할 수 있다.

(11) 오른쪽으로 돌면 당신은 그 건물을 발견할 것이다.

(12) 젊지만 그녀는 많은 경험을 가지고 있다.

(13) 경찰을 보자 그는 도망쳤다.

(14) 아버지가 집에 오시면 반드시 나에게 사탕을 좀 사오신다.

(15) 그 책이 재미있어서 그것은 잘 팔린다.

2. 다음 문장을 영작하시오.

(1) Walking along the street, I met her.

(2) It being rainy, I gave up going out.

(3) On hearing the news, he was surprised.

(4) But for your help, he could not succeed.

(5) I don't know where to go.

3. 다음 단문을 복문으로 바꾸시오.

(1) This is the man who writes an English book.

(2) I know the lady who is reading a newspaper in the room.

(3) This is the book which she should read.

(4) Can you tell me the reason why he should refuse the proposal?

(5) His father worked hard so that he might finish the work.

(6) He hurries so that he may not be late for school.

(7) She is so clever that she can understand the fact.

(8) She is so kind that she can show me the way to the post office.

(9) I should be happy if I could go abroad to study more.

(10) While I was playing tennis, I made a friend.

(11) As I have no money, I cannot lend him any.

(12) If you go to the park right now, you will meet her.

(13) Though I live in the apartment, I don't know Mr. Kim.

(14) If it is fine today, I will play tennis.

(15) When you choose a friend, you must be very careful.

(16) As soon as he saw me, he stood up and went out.

(17) Whenever my father comes home, he buys me some cake.

(18) My car leaves Seoul at six, and it arrives in Busan at eleven. (중문)

(19) I respect a person who is wise.

(20) The man who is honest will be loved by everyone.

1. 다음 영문을 우리말로 옮기시오.

(1) 그녀는 선생님이자 시인이었다고 한다.
(2) 그녀가 그런 남자와 결혼하지 않는 것은 당연하다.
(3) 그녀는 집을 사기 위해서 열심히 일했다.
(4) 그는 너무 나이가 많아서 자기 가족을 부양할 수 없다.
(5) 그 산은 너무 높아서 우리는 올라갈 수 없다.
(6) 그는 너무 지혜로워서 모든 이들이 그의 의견을 듣고 싶어 한다.
(7) 그는 열심히 일해서 많은 돈을 벌었다.
(8) 탁자 위에 있는 금시계는 그녀의 것이다.
(9) 테니스를 치고 있는 그 소년은 나의 형제이다.
(10) 그는 내가 웅변대회에서 상을 타야 한다고 주장했다.
(11) 그녀가 화를 낼 이유가 없다.
(12) 물이 없다면 우리는 더 이상 살 수 없을 텐데.
(13) 나는 바빠서 회의에 갈 수 없었다.
(14) 나는 숙제를 마치자 잠자리에 들었다.
(15) 나는 매우 추워서 외출하지 않았다.

2. 다음 문장을 영작하시오.

(1) It is believed that he is honest.
(2) As it was rainy, I stayed at home all day long.
(3) As I am too tired, I want to go to bed.
(4) I studied hard so that I might enter the college.
(5) She is proud that her daughter is a pianist.

3. 다음 복문을 단문으로 바꾸시오.

(1) She expects to get a job.
(2) She expects me to get a job.
(3) She expected to get a job.
(4) He seems to have been a writer.
(5) This is the man to teach us English.
(6) I know a boy playing baseball.
(7) The book written by Shakespeare is famous.
(8) I don't know what to do next.
(9) He did his best so as to make her happy.
(10) She was too tired to walk for a long time.
(11) The rock is too heavy for him to lift.

(12) She is kind enough to show me the way to the hospital.
(13) He is proud of being a musician.
(14) She is proud of her mother having been a famous pianist.
(15) The house on the hill is beautiful.
(16) I remember to send him some flowers.
(17) Having a lot of money, he can buy his son an airplane.
(18) It being rainy yesterday, I could not go to the party.
(19) On seeing me, he ran away.
(20) It is impossible for her to read the book through a week.

1. 다음 두 문장의 뜻이 같아지도록 밑줄 친 부분에 알맞은 말을 써 넣으시오.

(1) that he was diligent
(2) that he will come
(3) that came to the meeting
(4) who is playing baseball on the playground
(5) so difficult that she cannot read it
(6) While I was walking along the street
(7) As soon as he saw a police officer
(8) but she failed in the examination
(9) As he was ill
(10) Though it was raining heavily
(11) It seems that
(12) that I shall succeed
(13) in
(14) wise man
(15) I let him
(16) Because of the rain

시험에 강해지는

Academy Reading Mate

토마스 방 저 | 188*258mm | 252쪽 | 12,000원

30일만에 끝내는 즉석 영단어 3000

오규상 편저 | 128*188mm | 8,900원

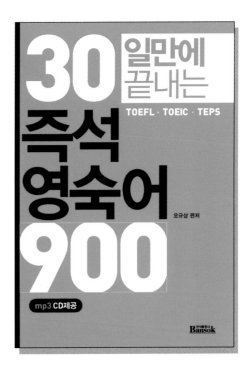

30일 만에 끝내는 즉석 영숙어 900

오규상 편저 | 128*188mm | 8,900원

초급 Junior Voca 3000

이홍배 지 | 188*258mm | 12,000원

왕초보 영어 단어장
WCB English Word Master

서지위, 장현애 저 | 148*210mm | 14,000원